W9-BNN-221

FOURTH EDITION

How to ADOPT YOUR STEPCHILD in California

By Frank Zagone & Attorney Mary Randolph

NOLO PRESS BERKELEY

YOUR RESPONSIBILITY WHEN USING A SELF-HELP LAW BOOK

We've done our best to give you useful and accurate information in this book. But laws and procedures change frequently and are subject to differing interpretations. If you want legal advice backed by a guarantee, see a lawyer. If you use this book, it's your responsibility to make sure that the facts and general advice contained in it are applicable to your situation.

KEEPING UP-TO-DATE

To keep its books up-to-date, Nolo Press issues new printings and new editions periodically. New printings reflect minor legal changes and technical corrections. New editions contain major legal changes, major text additions or major reorganizations. To find out if a later printing or edition of any Nolo book is available, call Nolo Press at (510) 549-1976 or check the catalog in the *Nolo News*, our quarterly newspaper.

To stay current, follow the "Update" service in the *Nolo News*. You can get the paper free by sending us the registration card in the back of this book. In another effort to help you use Nolo's latest materials, we offer a 25% discount off the purchase of any new Nolo book if you turn in any earlier printing or edition. (See the "Recycle Offer" in the front of the book.) This book was last revised in: **December 1993.**

FOURTH EDITION	January 1994
ILLUSTRATIONS	Arlene Tucker Zagone
PRODUCTION	Stephanie Harolde
BOOK DESIGN & LAYOUT	Toni Ihara
	Keija Kimura
	Jackie Mancuso
COVER ART	Miya Warner
PRINTING	Delta Lithograph

Zagone, Frank.
How to adopt your stepchild in California / by Frank Zagone & Mary Randolph. -- 4th California ed.
p. cm.
Includes index.
ISBN 0-87337-247-6 ; $22.95
1. Adoption--Law and legislation--California. 2. Stepchildren--Legal status, laws, etc.--California. 3. Adoption--Law and legislation--California--Forms. I. Randolph, Mary.
KFC 132.Z33 1994
346.79401 ' 78--dc20
[347.9406178]

94-2697
CIP

ACKNOWLEDGEMENTS

Thank you to:

My two children, Robin and Lisa, for their understanding when this project diverted my time from the family.

My wife, Arlene, for her artwork and encouragement.

Alma Tucker for her assistance in preparing the draft.

Marilyn Sanders and Gladys Lawton for help in draft preparation.

Jake Warner and Toni Ihara for their patient guidance on all phases of the book.

George Chaffey, Director, Legal Services Foundation, Contra Costa County, for his moral support.

Jon Johnsen, Richmond California Attorney, for his help and encouragement.

Various county employees for their help. My special thanks to Waleen Val Dez, an extremely capable and dedicated public worker.

DEDICATION

The idea for this book was originally promoted by the example of adoptive parents, Larry and Ruth, who have shown that love can run as thick as blood.

GET 25% OFF

YOUR NEXT PURCHASE

RECYCLE YOUR OUT-OF-DATE BOOKS

It's important to have the most current legal information. Because laws and legal procedures change often, we update our books regularly. To help keep you up-to-date we are extending this special offer. Cut out and mail the title portion of the cover of any old Nolo book with your next order and we'll give you a 25% discount off the retail price of ANY new Nolo book you purchase directly from us. For current prices and editions call us at 1-800-992-6656.

This offer is to individuals only.

CONTENTS

CHAPTER 5   ADOPTION BASED ON PARENT'S FAILURE TO SUPPORT CHILD

CHAPTER 6   ADOPTION BASED ON ABANDONMENT
BY THE ABSENT PARENT

Chapter 1

HOW TO USE THIS BOOK

If you are a California stepmother or stepfather wondering about what's involved in adopting your minor stepchild or stepchildren, this book is designed for you.

Here is what *How to Adopt Your Stepchild* does:

- It gives you practical and legal information to help you decide whether or not to adopt.

- It provides you with the information to determine if adoption is legally possible.

- Once you have decided that you want to adopt, it shows you, step-by-step, how to petition the court for adoption, acting as your own lawyer.

- It counsels you on how to get your case before a judge and what to say when you do.

- It alerts you to situations where a lawyer's help is necessary.

- For those of you who decide not to do your own adoption and instead hire a lawyer, it gives you the information necessary to understand what the lawyer is, or should be, doing.

To use this book effectively, read Chapters 1 and 2 for an overview of the adoption process. This includes understanding the preliminary steps you will have to take, how to work with court clerks and social service agency personnel, and how to request or prepare the documents you'll need. Then go to Chapter 3 to choose the correct stepparent adoption procedure. Next, read Chapter 4, 5, 6 or 7, depending on the kind of stepparent adoption procedure your situation mandates. Chapter 8 contains some hints about working with lawyers, if that's necessary. Tear-out copies of all the forms you need are included in the Appendix.

Even though California adoption laws apply to all counties in the state, the actual procedures by which papers are filled out and shuffled, court dates are set, and other details are handled may vary slightly from county to county. Even within a particular county, the procedural practice often includes small variations from time to time and from official to official. Thus, the procedures and steps we provide in this book may not always match exactly those used in your county. However, the variations, if any, will be minor and you should be able to adjust to them without difficulty. Most county workers will help you with local procedures not covered here once they see that you have the basic knowledge required to handle your own adoption.

 This book is designed only for simple, uncontested stepparent adoptions. It does *not* show you how to conduct a stepparent adoption proceeding in the following situations:

- The adoption is going to be contested by the absent parent.
- You want to adopt an adult (at least 18 years old) stepchild.
- You want to adopt a married minor stepchild.
- You are not married to the person whose child you want to adopt.

If you find yourself in any of these categories, consult an attorney.

Note on Name Changes: If you just want your stepchild's last name changed to yours, adoption is not necessary. You can change a child's name with a simple "Name Change Petition." A successful name change petition only changes the child's name. It doesn't make you the legal parent with the obligation to support the child, as adoption does. If what you are really interested in is a name change only, see *How to Change Your Name*, by attorneys David Loeb and David Brown (Nolo Press).

Chapter 2

Before You Adopt:
An Overview

Before you start filling out adoption forms, take a little while to familiarize yourself with the adoption process, as well as the legal and practical consequences of adopting a child.

A. Legal Consequences of Adoption

An adoption creates a legal parent-child relationship between the adopting parent and the stepchild. It gives both you and your stepchild many legal rights and responsibilities, some of which continue into the child's adulthood. Here are some of the more important aspects.

The law treats you as if your stepchild were your natural child. You become legally responsible for the care, education and support of the child until she is an adult (or even after, in some situations), and you have the right to exercise authority over the child. She has a child's right to inherit from you, if you die without a will. You have a corresponding right to inherit as a parent.

Your adopted child loses almost all child-parent rights with respect to the absent parent.[1] The child may, however, still inherit from the absent parent, if that parent dies without a will and the child and the absent parent ever lived together as parent and child. (Probate Code § 6408.) Of course, adoption doesn't affect wills; the absent parent could always leave your adopted child money or property by naming him in a will. Also, if the absent parent dies after the adoption, your adopted child may still be eligible to receive Social Security death benefits if the deceased absent parent had a Social Security account.

The absent parent loses all parental rights and obligations when his child is adopted. Thus he has no right to visit the child, and no obligation to provide support. The child is also relieved of any responsibilities he might have to the absent parent.

The changes in these rights are permanent. An adoption decree cannot be set aside unless there was a serious legal defect or fraud in the adoption action, or unless the adopted child is discovered to be developmentally disabled or mentally ill within five years after the adoption. (Family Code § 9100.)

DECIDING ABOUT ADOPTION

If you have not yet made a final decision as to whether to adopt, don't hesitate to ask yourself some tough questions:

- "If the absent parent is paying support, how will I feel when those payments stop after the adoption because he/she will no longer be responsible for child support?"

- "How will I feel about being legally responsible to help support my adopted child until he/she is grown, even if my spouse and I were to get a divorce?"

Or, if your stepchild is receiving public assistance (AFDC):

- "How will I feel when the AFDC financial assistance terminates after the adoption because my income disqualifies my adopted child from receiving aid?"

If you square off honestly with yourself, you will know when the time is right for adoption. If the time is never really right, it's better not to adopt.

---

[1] These rights are conferred by California's "intestate" succession laws. For an excellent explanation of intestate succession in California, see *How to Probate an Estate*, by Julia Nissley (Nolo Press).

B. Legal Requirements for Adoption

Before you begin the adoption process, make sure you meet these preliminary legal requirements:

1. Your spouse must be the legal parent of your stepchild and have the legal right to exclusive or joint custody of the child (see box below).

2. You, the adopting parent, must be at least eighteen years of age.

3. You must be legally married to your spouse.

4. You must have the consent of:

    a. Your spouse;

    b. The absent parent, unless he is deceased or the court rules that his consent is not necessary (see Chapters 5, 6 and 7); and

    c. Your stepchild, if he is 12 years of age or older.

5. You and the child's natural parent have been married for at least one year.[2]

After you file your petition for adoption, the adoption must be approved by:

- the Social Service Department (or other designated agency) of your county; and

- a judge of the Superior Court.

The Social Service Department (or court mediator, in some counties) will investigate the adoption and recommend that the court approve or disapprove it. As a practical matter, this "recommendation" is a virtual requirement for a successful adoption petition; courts seldom go against the agency's wishes.[3]

The Superior Court judge gives final approval to the adoption petition. The judge must find that the adoption serves the best interest of the child and that you are willing and able to care for and educate the child.

---

[2]This is a practical, not legal, requirement. See Chapter 4, Section C.

[3]Actual approval from Social Service is legally required if the absent parent lives outside of California or if the court rules that his consent is not required. Under those circumstances, Social Service in effect takes the place of the absent parent and must give consent. If the Social Service Department refuses its consent, you have the right to appeal to the court.

ESTABLISHING PARENTAL AND CUSTODY RIGHTS

Before a stepparent can adopt his spouse's child, he must show that his spouse is the legal parent, and has legal custody, of the child. If you don't think you can clearly show your spouse's legal parentage or legal right to have custody of your stepchild, help from a lawyer may be in order.

1. If You Are the Stepfather Who Wants to Adopt

Parentage. Your wife will probably have no difficulty in establishing herself as the legal parent (even if her child was born out of wedlock), as long as there is a recorded birth certificate naming her the mother. If she is the adoptive mother, again there is probably no problem.[4]

Custody. Being a legal parent is not necessarily proof that one has a legal right to custody of the child. A mother living with her child probably has legal custody if:

- She is divorced from the legal father and has a court order giving her sole or joint custody; or

- She is divorced from the legal father, who has a court order granting him legal custody but has voluntarily agreed to her having actual custody; or

- She became the sole custodian when the legal father died; or

- She became the sole custodian when the legal father lost his legal parentage through legal proceedings; or

- The child was born to her out-of-wedlock, and there is no court order affecting custody of the child.

2. If You Are the Stepmother Who Wants to Adopt

Paternity. Your spouse will probably not have difficulty in showing himself to be the legal father of his child if the child was born in wedlock and there is a recorded birth certificate naming him as the father. If he is the adoptive father, again he shouldn't have trouble proving his status.[5]

---

[4]These examples assume that her legal parentage was never terminated through court action.

[5]These examples assume that his legal parentage was never terminated through court action.

A man whose child was born out of wedlock, and who has no court order declaring him to be the father, may have some problems in proving his legal status as father. He will be presumed to be the father, and any problems proving his legal status as father should be surmountable if:

- his name appeared on the birth certificate,
- he lived with the mother after the birth of the child and acknowledged that it was his,
- he signed a paternity statement, or
- he married the mother after the birth of the child.

Custody. Assuming your spouse is the legal parent of his child as outlined above, and he is living with his child, he probably has legal custody if:

- He is divorced from (or was never married to) the legal mother, and he has a court order giving him sole or joint custody; or
- He is divorced from (or was never married to) the legal mother, who has a court order granting her custody but has voluntarily agreed to his having actual custody; or
- He became the sole custodian when the legal mother died; or
- He became the sole custodian when the legal mother lost her legal parentage through court action.

Note: If your husband does not have a court order giving him custody and the natural mother is missing, he must be prepared to explain to the court that the mother voluntarily agreed to his having actual custody or to present some other valid explanation as to the circumstances under which he got custody of the child.

C. THE ADOPTION PROCESS

In California, there are three main types of procedures for adopting a stepchild. Which one you will follow depends on the circumstances in your family. Here is a brief description of each.

IMPORTANT DEFINITIONS

One of the terms you will see quite a bit in this book is "absent parent." If you are a stepmother, "absent parent" means the legal mother of your stepchild. If you are a stepfather, it means the legal father of your stepchild.

The term "missing parent" is used for an absent parent whose whereabouts are unknown.

If the absent parent consents: If your stepchild's absent parent consents to the adoption or is deceased, the process should be smooth and quick. You will file an adoption petition with the Superior Court for your county, talk to a local Social Service agency, go to a short hearing in front of a judge, and file the adoption decree with the county clerk. (Chapter 4)

If you can't find the absent parent: If your stepchild's absent parent can't be located, the process is a little more complicated. You first must try to locate the missing parent. You may need to claim, in documents filed with the court, that the absent parent abandoned the child or willfully failed to meet his parental obligations. The County Social Service Department and the court must approve the adoption. (Chapters 5, 6 and 7)

If the absent parent won't consent: If your stepchild's absent parent won't consent to the adoption, you may not be able to adopt your stepchild. A legal parent who is in contact with and supports the child and contests the adoption petition can prevent the adoption. If the absent parent won't consent but doesn't actually contest the adoption petition in court, you may still be able to adopt. (Chapter 4)

D. REPRESENTING YOURSELF

It's legally permissible to represent yourself in court without a lawyer. The technical term for this is "In Propria Persona" (or "In Pro Per"), which means "on one's own behalf." You indicate that you are handling your legal action yourself simply by placing your name, address, and phone number followed by "Petitioner In Pro Per" at the upper left of the petition and other documents you file with the court. Our sample documents show you how.

As stated in Chapter 1, if the stepparent adoption is likely to be contested by the absent parent, you should consult a lawyer and not rely on this book.

1. Documents to Collect

Before you start stepparent adoption proceedings, collect the following documents, which you will need to give to the county Social Service Department.[6]

- A certified copy of your stepchild's birth certificate (that is, a copy from the county recorder's office)

- Marriage certificates of:

  1. your present marriage

  2. all your prior marriages

  3. all your spouse's prior marriages.

- Final judgments of Dissolution of Marriage (Divorce Decrees) of all

  1. your prior marriages

  2. your spouse's prior marriages.

- Any court order awarding custody of your stepchild to your spouse. This is usually contained in the Interlocutory Judgment of Dissolution of Marriage for California divorces granted before July 1, 1984 and in the final judgment dissolution for divorces granted after that date.

- Death Certificate(s) if, during a prior marriage, you or your spouse became a widow or widower.

- Military discharge papers of you or your spouse.

- Your social security number and that of your spouse.

Although usually a file-stamped copy is sufficient, some Social Service agencies ask for "certified" copies of some, or all, of the documents. A certified copy is one which has been stamped or embossed with a seal by the court or agency which issues the original document. The certification indicates that the copy is a true reproduction of the original on file with the court or agency.

When you need a certified copy of a document for Social Service, but you only have a file-endorsed or other non-certified copy, send a photocopy of the copy you have to the issuer with a request for a certified copy. There is usually a small fee charged for each certified copy. This varies with the agency and the number of pages you need copied. If the issuing court or agency is nearby, you might want to make a phone call to find out what the fee will be. You can then enclose the exact amount with your request letter. In the case of California court documents, the fee to certify each copy or set usually runs between $4 and $11,

---

[6]By the time you have finished your adoption, you will have collected an impressive array of papers, including all sorts of certified copies of records, and file-endorsed copies of court documents. Now is the time to set up a good, safe record keeping system. For suggestions on how to go about this, see *Nolo's Personal RecordKeeper*, a software package from Nolo Press.

and the fee for each photocopied page is around $1 or $2. The fee for a certified copy of a birth, marriage or death certificate is commonly from $5 to $15.

If the court or agency is far away or in another state, you can send a check or money order for a reasonable amount (say $25) requesting the return of any unneeded amount. Or you can send a check payable to the court or agency but with no amount written in. In a clear area on the check, write in "Not to Exceed Fifteen Dollars." Adjust the amount upward or downward depending on the number of certified copies and number of pages you want.

Have your spouse sign the request if the document pertains to her or to your stepchild.

Your letter might go something like this:

SAMPLE LETTER TO CLERK

February 3, 19__

Clerk of the Superior Court (Civil)
County of San Joaquin
123 West St.
Stockton, California 97890

Dear Clerk:

Enclosed is a photocopy of my Final Judgment of Dissolution of Marriage. Please send me two certified copies in the enclosed addressed and stamped envelope.

Since I do not know the amount of your fee, I have enclosed a check not to exceed twenty dollars. Please fill in the exact amount. Thank you.

Very truly yours,

David Kramer
9864 Leonard Street
Stockton, CA 98765
(501) 776-9853

Enclosures

2. Working With the Social Service Department

A county agency always makes a recommendation to the court on a stepparent adoption. In most counties, the Probation Department conducts an investigation and makes the report. In some counties, however, the Welfare Department (sometimes called the Social Service Department) handles the job. Throughout this book we use the term Social Service Department to mean whatever county department performs the assessment function.

WHO HANDLES STEPPARENT ADOPTIONS

Stepparent adoptions are processed by the county Welfare or Probation Department. The Probation Department handles them *except* in these counties:

Alameda	Placer	Stanislaus
Contra Costa	San Bernardino	Tuolumne
Mendocino	Santa Cruz	Ventura
Monterey	Shasta	

In Los Angeles County, there is a special agency, the Department of Adoptions. And in Butte County, the Family Conciliation Court is in charge.

The investigation is not an adversary process. The social worker who is in charge of your adoption will talk to you and your family, and probably ask for some information and references. He won't be looking for reasons to disapprove the adoption. The process is discussed more fully in Chapter 4.

3. Preparing and Filing Court Documents

You, the petitioner, will have to type out all the documents required by the court in the course of the adoption proceedings.

a. Typing Your Documents

Most courts require the petition for adoption, adoption decree and any other documents you file to be typed on 8-1/2" x 11" numbered legal paper. Some, however, accept plain paper; you can call the court clerk and ask. Do not use 14"-length paper; the courts no longer accept it. Numbered legal paper is available at most office supply stores and is an option with some word processing software.

It's okay to use white touch-up correction fluid to correct typing errors. Keep your lines lined up with the numbers on the legal paper.

Below is a sample of a completed petition to show you how a ready-to-file document should look. The same heading layout is used on all documents you file with the court. Of course, the titles of the individual documents are different, and the caption (that is, the part that begins: In The Matter of. . .) will vary. Pay close attention to the caption on the sample forms we show you.

Stepmother Adoptions. Since stepfather adoptions far outnumber stepmother adoptions, we have worded the samples in this book as though the petitioner is a stepfather. If you are a stepmother, before you start to type the document, go over the wording in the sample and reverse the gender where appropriate.

Example:

```
"Petitioner is the wife of _____, who is
the father of the minor and who has custody of the minor.
Petitioner, her spouse and the minor reside in
_____ County, California."
```

More Than One Stepchild. The sample forms are also worded as though you are adopting only one stepchild. If you are adopting more than one stepchild, go over the sample forms you will need, pluralizing the appropriate words before typing your document. You may use one petition to request adoption of more than one child if the children all have the same two parents. If your stepchildren have different absent parents (for example, your wife had a child with each of her two former husbands), you will need to file separate petitions.

Here are several very important points to keep in mind as you prepare your documents:

1. Always type: SUPERIOR COURT OF CALIFORNIA on line 8 and COUNTY OF [YOUR COUNTY] on line 9.

2. Always start typing the body of the document on line 13.

3. Always type your first, middle, and last name (*no* initials) in the caption.

4. Always type your name, address, phone number and "Petitioner In Pro Per" in the extreme upper left.

5. Always type in the verification statement at the end of any petition. (See the sample petition.)

Be as accurate as you can in preparing your documents. Have someone double-check your selection of forms and check your wording against the sample form.

After preparing a form, make three good photocopies of it. Do not sign the document until after you have made the photocopies; then sign each copy individually.

One last word about forms: If, after you file your document, you discover that you made a serious mistake or omission in the wording, prepare and file an amended document with the needed corrections. See Section d below.

b. Which Court to File In

The court that will handle your adoption case is the Superior Court located in the county in which you live. All documents in connection with your adoption action have to be filed with the clerk of the Superior Court. Since in many counties the county clerk also functions as the Clerk of the Superior Court, we use the term "county clerk" as synonymous with "Clerk of the Superior Court." However, when you communicate with the county about your adoption action, use the term "Clerk of the Superior Court (Civil)" so it will know that you are referring to a civil (not criminal) court matter.

Even though the county clerk is an individual, we use the term in this book to refer to a county department. The actual human whom you will deal with will probably have the title "Deputy County Clerk."

Look in the phone book under "County Offices" to get the address of the county clerk's office, which is often located in the county courthouse. If your county has courthouse/county clerk branches in different parts of the county, communicate with the office closest to you.

PETITION FOR ADOPTION

1	JOHN LEE DOE 560 West Street
2	Sacramento, California 96540 Phone: (515) 123-4567
3	Petitioner In Pro Per
4	
5	
6	
7	
8	SUPERIOR COURT OF CALIFORNIA
9	COUNTY OF SACRAMENTO
10	
11	In the Matter of the Adoption Petition) No._____
12	of JOHN LEE DOE, Adopting Parent) PETITION FOR ADOPTION _____) (Stepparent)
13	JOHN LEE DOE, Petitioner, alleges:
14	1. The name by which the minor who is the subject of this petition
15	was registered at birth is Mary Jane Smith.
16	2. The minor child is a female born on June 5, 1981, in San Jose,
17	California.
18	3. Petitioner is an adult person and desires to adopt the minor
19	child. Petitioner is the husband of June Amy Doe, who is the mother of
20	the child and who has custody of the child. Petitioner, his spouse and
21	the minor child reside in Sacramento County, California.
22	4. The mother of the child, June Amy Doe, was married to Petitioner
23	on July 10th, 1985, at Sacramento, California and is prepared to consent
24	to the minor's adoption by Petitioner, retaining all her rights of
25	custody and control.
26	5. The natural father and mother of the minor were married in San
27	Francisco, California on March 3, 1978. The marriage was terminated on
28	August 7, 1982 by Superior Court of California, County of San Francisco

-1-

1   in proceeding number 35423. The father is prepared to consent to the

2   adoption by Petitioner.

3   6. The child is a proper subject for adoption, and Petitioner is

4   willing and able to care for the child properly. The child's best inter-

5   ests will be promoted by this adoption. Petitioner agrees to adopt the

6   child and treat the child in all respects as his own lawful child.

7   WHEREFORE, Petitioner prays that the Court grant this petition and

8   decree that the child has been legally adopted by Petitioner, and that

9   Petitioner and child shall thenceforth sustain toward each other the

10   legal relation of parent and child with all rights and duties of that

11   relation, and that the child shall be known as Mary Jane Doe.

12   _____

13   Petitioner

14

15

16   <u>VERIFICATION</u>

17   The statements in the above Petition are true of my own knowledge,

18   except as to the matters that are therein stated on my information and

19   belief, and as to those matters I believe them to be true.

20   Executed on June 5, 19__, at Sacramento, California.

21   I declare under penalty of perjury that the foregoing is true and

22   correct.

23   _____

24   Petitioner

25

26

27

28

c. How to File Documents

You file a document simply by handing it across the counter at the county clerk's office with a request that it be filed. When you file your adoption petition (your first court paper), the clerk will assign a case number and place it on the first page. You put this case number on all later papers you file. You will be required to refer to this number in all communications with the clerk's office.

When you file a document, give the county clerk the original and three photocopies. The clerk keeps the original for the court file. The clerk may keep one photocopy too, depending on county policy. The rest of the photocopies are given back to you immediately, each rubber-stamped in the upper right-hand corner to show that the original was filed. The case number and the date of filing will also be stamped on each photocopy returned. These rubber-stamped photocopies are called "file-endorsed copies." Assuming you make three photocopies of each form filed, you should wind up getting back either two or three rubber-stamped copies of each document.

If you want a file-endorsed copy to be "certified," that is, stamped or embossed with a special seal to authenticate the document, just ask the clerk when you file it, and pay the small fee.

Note: A photocopy of a file-endorsed copy is not a file-endorsed copy and should not be represented as one. The same is true of a photocopy of a certified copy.

Note on Filing by Mail: You can mail documents you want to file to the clerk, but we don't recommend it. Aside from the obvious danger of delay or loss in the mails, it can be very helpful to go in person and establish a good relationship with the clerk's office staff, whom you will be dealing with later.

d. Amending or Withdrawing Filed Documents

When you file a petition or other document and later find it necessary to correct a serious error or change its wording, you can file an amended document. You use the same title as the original document except that you use the term "AMENDED," e.g., "AMENDED PETITION," "AMENDED DECREE OF ADOPTION," etc. You then file the original and copies of amended document, with the changed wording, with the county clerk in the same manner as you did the original document, getting back rubber-stamped photocopies.

Example: You file a petition to adopt without the consent of the missing parent under one of the grounds discussed in Chapter 3. The petition makes reference to the grounds for adopting without the consent of the missing parent. After filing your petition you make contact with the missing parent, who then signs a consent form. Now you must prepare an amended petition, which states that the absent parent consents, and file it with the county clerk.

Another reason to file an amended document would be your discovery of a serious error on the original document after you filed it.

If for some reason you don't want to go through with the adoption hearing and wish to withdraw the petition, you must ask the county clerk for a "REQUEST FOR DISMISSAL" form, fill it out and file it with the county clerk.

Example 1: You have filed a petition to terminate parental rights of the alleged father together with the adoption petition (Chapter 7). You later obtain the consent of the alleged father so there is no need to have the termination of rights hearing. You withdraw the termination of rights petition by filing a Request for Dismissal form. You also file an amended adoption petition stating that the absent parent consents.

Example 2: You filed to adopt without the consent of the missing parent. Later the missing parent surfaces with full intention of contesting your action. You decide to withdraw your petition.

E. CHANGING YOUR ADOPTED CHILD'S NAME

As part of the adoption, your stepchild's last name can be changed to any name on which you, your spouse and your stepchild all agree. Many people choose to have the child's last name changed to the adoptive father's, though you can use a last name that has no connection with either your name or your spouse's. To change your stepchild's name, put the new name in the adoption decree; the change becomes legally effective when the decree is filed with the court.

You can have the child's birth certificate amended to reflect the new name. Whether or not your stepchild's name is being changed, the birth certificate can still be changed to show you as the parent. (See Chapter 5, Section H.) The name of the absent parent is removed and you are shown as the parent. No mention is made in the new birth certificate of the adoption; the certificate will appear the same as it would if you were the natural parent. The old birth certificate is sealed and can only be unsealed by a court order.

An amended birth certificate is not required by law, even if your stepchild's name is changed on the adoption decree. But most people, thinking of the confusing situations that may arise for a stepchild in later years, choose to have the birth certificate changed if the stepchild's name is changed. Since you, your spouse, and your stepchild (if she if old enough to reason) have quite a bit of leeway regarding the name change and birth certificate, you may wish to kick around the pros and cons in a three-way conference.

Chapter 3

CHOOSING THE CORRECT
STEPPARENT ADOPTION PROCEDURE

The procedure you will follow to adopt your stepchild depends, in large part, on the absent parent. If the absent parent isn't available or won't consent, your adoption will involve more work. In some instances, adoption may even be impossible. This chapter tells you how to select the procedure you need.

A. IF THE ABSENT PARENT CONSENTS

If the absent parent consents to the adoption, the process is relatively quick and simple. You can skip this chapter and go to Chapter 4, which contains instructions and forms.

Out-of-wedlock births: If your stepchild was born out-of-wedlock, the natural father can give his consent without admitting paternity. (See Chapter 4.)

B. IF YOU CAN'T FIND THE ABSENT PARENT

If you, your stepchild and your spouse are all in favor of adoption, but you can't find the absent parent to get his consent, you can probably adopt without the missing parent's consent on one of three legal grounds:

1. Willful failure by the missing parent to support the child. (Family Code § 8604.)

2. Abandonment by the missing parent. (Family Code § 7822.)

3. Out-of-wedlock birth—no "presumed" father. (Family Code § 7611.)

You must be able to prove one of these grounds. The law is very protective of a natural parent's legal relationship. Only when the parent fails to exercise the responsibilities that go along with this right—to communicate with or support his child—will the courts allow interference. If there is any doubt about your ability to prove the facts, or if you are unsure whether or not sufficient grounds exist, see a lawyer.[1]

1. Willful Failure by Missing Parent to Support Child

A legal parent's consent to adoption is not required if that parent "for a period of one year willfully fails to communicate with and to pay for the care, support, and education of the child when able to do so." (Family Code § 8604.) (Section 3 below explains how to determine whether or not the father of a child born out-of-wedlock is presumed to be the legal father.)

To use the "willful failure" ground for adoption, your spouse must have custody of your stepchild by court order or by "agreement of the parents." If your spouse does not have a court order for custody, think about how you are going to convince the court that the missing parent agreed to give your spouse custody. This should not be too difficult if the missing parent is not going to contest.

How do you prove to the court that the failure of the missing parent to support and communicate was "willful"? As long as the missing parent has not communicated with and has not supported the child for a one-year period, the court will presume "willfulness" absent a satisfactory explanation. If you have any reason to believe the missing parent can come up with a convincing explanation for not supporting and communicating with the child, see a lawyer before petitioning.

Sometimes, you may be able to proceed using either this ground or the abandonment ground (Section 2 below). An abandonment action may be preferable if the stepchild was born out of wedlock, because some judges

---

[1] There are some additional grounds (for example, mental illness of one parent) that are not included in our discussion. Because of the specialized nature of these other grounds, you should see a lawyer if you want to use them.

consider the "willful failure" ground in Section 8604 appropriate only when the natural parents were married. Before you make a final decision, you may want to check with your local Social Service agency to see which approach is best in your situation.

2. Abandonment by the Missing Parent

If a court decides that the absent parent has legally "abandoned" your stepchild, only your spouse's consent to the adoption will be required. Abandonment, under the law, means that the absent parent has intentionally not supported or not communicated with the child for more than a year. (Family Code § 7822.)

You may want to petition using the abandonment ground because:

- In abandonment actions, you only need to show either failure to communicate or failure to support, whereas in "willful failure" cases you need to prove both of these elements. Thus, if the absent parent has failed to provide any support over a one-year period but has communicated on a regular basis with the stepchild, you can still use the abandonment law but will be unable to establish "willful failure" under Section 8604.

- A Probation Department investigation is automatic in abandonment actions. You may wish to have the benefit of the department's report to convince the court of the missing parent's neglect of parental responsibilities. In "willful failure" actions, there is just the testimony of the parties.

- If the natural parents were not married and there is no court order granting custody, most Superior Courts recommend an abandonment action instead of a willful failure action.[2]

Example: Your spouse is divorced from the absent parent, Gary. After the divorce Gary moved to another part of the state. In the last three years he has not communicated with your spouse or the child. When the District Attorney contacted Gary after the first year of disappearance, Gary made support payments directly to the county for two months. During the next two-year period, he made support payments to County Collections twice in each year, but only after being contacted by the D.A.'s office. The D.A. is now unable to locate him. It has been six months since the last support payment was made to County Collections.

In this example, the situation has some elements of abandonment but is not clear-cut. The determination as to whether or not the absent parent legally abandoned his child would depend on the Probation Department investigation and the opinion of the judge.

---

[2]The willful failure action was intended for situations in which the parents were married. When it was created by the legislature, the consent of an absent parent wasn't even needed for adoption unless the parents had been married when the child was born.

Before filing an abandonment petition, you should discuss your intention to file with the Social Service Department or County Probation Department. They may indicate that the court in your county prefers the willful failure (Section 1 above) approach. You may also want to consult an attorney experienced in adoptions.

COMPARING "WILLFUL FAILURE" AND ABANDONMENT" PROCEEDINGS

"Willful Failure"—Section 8604

- There is only one petition and one hearing, where both thequestion of eliminating the need for the missing parent's consent and the question of adoption itself are decided by the court.

- The court's decision is based on the Social Service assessmentand the petitioner's testimony that the missing parent willfully failed to meet his parental obligations.

- The absent parent is given notice of the hearing by a citation,ordering him to appear at the hearing.

Abandonment—Section 7822

- Two petitions and two court orders (one on the abandonment, one on the adoption) are required. Both hearings are held at the same time.

- The County Probation Department makes an investigation of thealleged abandonment and submits an opinion to the court. Thecourt refers to the Probation Department report, as well as to yourtestimony, in arriving at a decision.

- If the missing parent can't be given notice of the hearing personally, a citation (ordering him to appear at the hearing) is published in a newspaper. The petitioner must also notify certain relatives of the missing parent about the abandonment hearing.

3. Termination of Missing Father's Rights— Out-of-Wedlock Birth

If your child was born out of wedlock and you can't find the natural father, you may be able to file a petition to terminate the parental rights of the missing father. Once the father's rights are terminated, his consent is not necessary to the adoption.

You can file such a petition if:

- The child was born out of wedlock, and

- No one is presumed, under law, to be the child's legal father.

If no one is legally presumed to be the child's father, the natural father is known as the "alleged" father.

If your stepchild has a presumed father, you must either get his consent to the adoption or proceed under a "willful failure" (Section 1 above) or abandonment (Section 2 above) ground.

First, then, you must determine whether or not the law presumes anyone to be your stepchild's father. A man is presumed to be the father of a child born out-of-wedlock if:

- He and the child's mother were married before the child was born, and the child was born within 300 days after the marriage ended or a decree of separation was entered by a court.

- He and the child's mother attempted to marry before the child's birth, but the marriage was (or could have been) declared invalid, and the child was born within 300 days of when the marriage ended or the parties quit living together; or

- He and the child's mother attempted to marry after the child's birth, but the marriage is or could be declared invalid, and

  —he is named, with his consent, on the birth certificate, or

  —he is obligated (by promise or court order) to support the child; or

- He receives the child into his home and openly holds out the child as his own, or

- The child was born and resides outside the United States and the father signs a declaration under penalty of perjury that he is the father.

Paternity Statements: Paternity statements (that is, a signed statement in which a man declares that he is the father of a certain child) are not specifically mentioned in the statute. If the father has signed a paternity statement, however, he could be considered to have "held out the child as his own." The decision would be up to the judge.

These presumptions, found in Family Code § 7611, can be rebutted by "clear and convincing" evidence that the absent parent is not the father or by a court decree establishing that another man is the father.

Keep in mind that the determination of whether or not the natural father is the "presumed" father does not depend on what the mother says. For example, the mother may identify a man as the natural father of her out-of-wedlock child, but the law may not give to him "presumed" father status because the birth circumstances do not fall within Section 7611 and a paternity statement has not been signed.

Example 1: Your wife and the natural father of your stepchild were not living together at the time of the child's birth or at any time after the birth. They never had a wedding ceremony, and the natural father's name is not on the birth certificate. The natural father never offered to support the child or signed a paternity statement.

Under these circumstances, the natural father is only the "alleged," not "presumed," father. A termination of parental rights action would be the appropriate action, or, if the alleged father signs a "Denial of Paternity," you could use the procedures for a consent adoption (Chapter 4).

Example 2: Your wife and the natural father of your stepchild, although not married, lived together before and after the birth. The natural father's name appeared on the birth certificate, and he told all of his friends and relatives that the baby was his.

In this situation, he is the legally presumed father. Termination of his parental rights would not be the appropriate action. To adopt the child, you would need to either get the presumed father's consent or proceed under an abandonment or "willful failure to support" theory.

4. What If the Missing Parent Surfaces?

If you file a petition to adopt without the consent of the missing parent because you don't know his address, and later you discover his whereabouts, you will need to:

1. Notify Social Service.

2. Ask the missing parent for his consent to the adoption.

3. If he agrees to consent, prepare and file an amended petition (see Chapter 2, Section D), and follow the procedures in Chapter 4.

4. If the absent parent refuses to consent, follow the procedures in Section B below.

C. WHAT IF THE ABSENT PARENT REFUSES TO CONSENT TO THE ADOPTION?

As we pointed out in Chapter 1, when you know the whereabouts of the absent legal parent, he is meeting his legal responsibilities to support or visit the child, and he refuses to give his consent, you have a problem. The law absolutely protects the legal rights of the natural parent in this situation. You cannot adopt the child of a natural parent who supports and stays in contact with his child and opposes the adoption.

1. Absent Parent Intends to Contest the Adoption

If you are convinced the absent parent will legally contest the adoption, but you also believe that his failure to support or contact the child gives you grounds for the adoption, you should see a lawyer. A lawyer may be able to accomplish the adoption in spite of the absent parent's refusal to cooperate.

2. Absent Parent Won't Contest the Adoption

What if the absent parent refuses to consent, but you are convinced that he will not contest the adoption in court? If you know you have grounds to adopt without his consent, you may wish to go ahead, filing an adoption petition under one of the three grounds discussed in Section A. If there is no contest, you're all set. You are on the way to getting the adoption and have saved yourself the attorney's fee. If the absent parent does oppose the adoption petition, you haven't lost much. You can still hire an attorney or withdraw your petition.

If you are filing under Section 8604 ("willful failure") and know where the absent parent is, the Social Service Department may be unwilling to submit a favorable recommendation without a signed consent from the absent parent. Check with Social Service before you file. If Social Service is unwilling to submit a favorable recommendation without the absent parent's consent, your only recourse is to petition under Section 7822 (abandonment). Social Service is often more willing to file a favorable recommendation after the Probation Department files a report showing the facts of the abandonment.

Chapter 4

ADOPTION IF THE ABSENT PARENT CONSENTS

The most straightforward kind of stepparent adoption occurs when the absent parent consents. Obviously, if everybody agrees, you should be able to run through the adoption procedure with a minimum of trouble.

Here's a brief outline of the process if you have the absent parent's consent:

1. Collect supporting documents (birth and marriage certificates, etc.; the entire list is in Chapter 2, Section D).

2. Get the absent parent's informal consent.

3. Prepare and file a petition for adoption.

4. Cooperate with your county social service agency as it investigates your adoption petition.

5. Arrange for the absent parent to sign a formal consent.

6. Attend a brief hearing with a judge, and file the decree of adoption.

That's it. These steps are discussed below. A detailed checklist is included at the end of the chapter.

A. CONSENT

Once you have gathered the documents listed in Chapter 2, Section D, you are ready to move on to the next step—getting the consents that will make the adoption a simple procedure.

1. Whose Consent Do You Need?

a. Parents

Both legal parents of the child must consent, in writing, to the adoption. Obviously, the consent of the parent to whom you are married should not be a problem. It's only the absent parent's consent that need concern you.

CHILDREN BORN OUT-OF-WEDLOCK

If the child was born out-of-wedlock, the absent parent's consent is still required unless:

- the identity of the absent parent is unknown; or

- the absent parent is not legally presumed to be the child's father (see Chapter 3, Section A3).

Even if you do not need the consent of the biological father, who is technically referred to as an "alleged father," the adoption process will be simpler if you get his consent. It even makes sense to get the consents of two or more men if either could be the natural father and there is no presumed father.

Sometimes an alleged father has no objection to the adoption, but nevertheless refuses to sign a consent because he fears that by doing so, he will be admitting he is the father and will expose himself to legal liability for past unpaid child support. If this is the case, instead of signing a consent form, he can sign either a "Waiver of Notice" to a hearing or a "Denial of Paternity" (available from your Social Service Department). If he signs either of these documents, he does not admit paternity, but you can proceed as though you have a signed consent form.

---

b. The Child

A child who is 12 or older must also consent to the stepparent adoption in writing. Although consent of a child under 12 is not legally required, the Social

Service Department and the judge will take into account the child's wishes when they decide whether or not to approve the adoption.

2. How Do You Get Consent?

a. Informal Consent

You don't need signed consent forms until after you file the adoption petition. (In fact, the consent form should not be signed until after the petition has been filed.) Before you file the petition, it is sufficient to have informal consent—that is, expressions by your spouse, the absent parent and your stepchild that convince you that they intend to sign formal consent forms when the time comes.

In approaching the absent parent, a straightforward request for consent will probably let you know where you stand. Write or say something like this: "I would like your consent to my adopting Lisa. Both Lisa and her mother are in favor of it. Will you think it over?"

If the absent parent wants information on the legal consequences, you might offer to pay for him to get a half-hour to an hour consultation from an attorney of his choice. It is to your advantage for the absent parent to give his consent after having fully considered the matter and without any pressure from you, your spouse or your stepchild.

b. Formal Written Consent

The absent parent must sign a formal statement of consent in the presence of certain witnesses designated by law. How to arrange this is discussed in Section D below.

The stepchild, if he is 12 or older, must also formally consent to the adoption by signing a consent form (part of the Adoption Agreement) in the presence of the judge at the adoption hearing.

B. PREPARING AND FILING THE ADOPTION PETITION

Okay, let's assume you've made an assessment of the legal requirements for adoption (Chapter 2, Section B) and you're convinced you can meet them. You know your stepchild and your spouse vote "yes." The absent parent has given you the go-ahead. Everything checks out and you are ready to begin your solo flight—that is, you are ready to petition the court "In Pro Per."

The adoption petition is a formal request directed to the county Superior Court. You are requesting the court to issue an order (called a "decree") making you the legal parent of your stepchild. Since you, the stepparent, are the one asking the court to let you adopt, you are called the "petitioner."

In the petition, you point out that each legal requirement for the adoption has or can be met. You include:

- The name, birthdate and sex of each child to be adopted. (As mentioned earlier, you can use one petition to adopt more than one stepchild, as long as the children all have the same two natural parents.)

- Your name and that of your spouse, where and when you were married, and the county of your residence.

- The name of the absent parent, where and when he and your spouse were married, and where and when their marriage was dissolved. (Or indicate that the child was born out of wedlock or that the absent parent died while married to your spouse.)

Here is a sample petition, with instructions on how to prepare your own. General instructions for typing court documents are in Chapter 2, Section D.

PETITION FOR ADOPTION

```
 1   [YOUR FULL NAME (In Capitals)]
     [Address]
 2   [City, State, Zip]
     [Your Phone No.]
 3   Petitioner In Pro Per

 4

 5

 6

 7

 8                    SUPERIOR COURT OF CALIFORNIA

 9                    COUNTY OF [Your County]

10   In the Matter of the          )   No. [Case No.]
     Adoption Petition of          )
11   [YOUR FULL NAME (In Capitals)], )   PETITION FOR ADOPTION
     Adopting Parent               )   (Stepparent)
12   _____ )

13      [Your Name], Petitioner, alleges:

14      1. The name by which the minor who is the subject of this petition

15   was registered at birth is [Full name of your stepchild as it appears on

16   birth certificate]. [See Instruction 1 below.]

17      2. The minor child is a [Male or Female] born on [Birthdate of your

18   stepchild] in [City and state of birth].

19      3. Petitioner is an adult person and desires to adopt the minor

20   child. Petitioner is the husband of [Full name of your wife], who is the

21   mother of the child and who has custody of the child. Petitioner, his

22   spouse and the minor child reside in [Your county] County, California.

23      4. The mother of the child, [Full name of your wife], was married

24   to Petitioner on [Date you and your wife were married] at [City and

25   state where you and your wife were married] and is prepared to consent

26   to the minor's adoption by Petitioner, retaining all her rights of

27   custody and control.

28   ////////
```

-1-

1 5. [See Instruction 2 below.]

2 6. The child is a proper subject for adoption, and Petitioner is

3 willing and able to care for the child properly. The child's best inter-

4 ests will be promoted by this adoption. Petitioner agrees to adopt the

5 child and treat the child in all respects as his own lawful child.

6 7. [See Instruction 3 below.]

7 WHEREFORE, Petitioner prays that the Court grant this petition and

8 decree that the child has been legally adopted by Petitioner, and that

9 Petitioner and child shall thenceforth sustain toward each other the

10 legal relation of parent and child with all rights and duties of that

11 relation and that the child shall be known as [New name]. [If your stepchild's

12 name is not being changed, end the sentence after the word "relation."]

13

14 [Your Signature] _____
    Petitioner

15

16

17

18

19 VERIFICATION

20 The statements in the above Petition are true of my own knowledge,

21 except as to the matters that are therein stated on my information and

22 belief, and as to those matters I believe them to be true.

23 Executed on _____, 19__, at _____, California.

24 I declare under penalty of perjury that the foregoing is true and

25 correct.

26 _____
    Petitioner

27

28

-2-

Petition for Adoption Instructions

1. If the child's name was changed after birth, add this at the end of paragraph 1:

Thereafter, the child's name was changed to [changed name] pursuant to [court, order number, date].

2. In paragraph 5, you need to say the absent parent will consent. If the marriage of your wife and the natural father ended by divorce, dissolution, or annulment, type in this: The natural mother and father of the minor were married in [City and State] on [Date]. The marriage was terminated on [Final Judgment of Dissolution Date] in [Name of Court] in proceeding No. [Judgment Number]. The father is prepared to consent to the adoption by Petitioner.

If your stepchild was born out-of-wedlock, type in this: The natural father and mother of the minor were never married. The natural father is prepared to consent to the adoption of the minor by Petitioner.

If the natural father died, type in this: The father of the minor died on [date], and only the consent of the mother is required for the adoption.

3. If your stepchild is 12 or older, add this: The child is prepared to consent to [his/her] adoption by Petitioner.

 These instructions and the sample are worded as though you are a stepfather. If you are a stepmother, when you type the petition, change the words father to mother, mother to father, wife to husband, and husband to wife. Also watch out for his, hers, him, and her.

 LOS ANGELES COUNTY NOTE.
Petitions filed in Los Angeles County must include information on your previous marriages. Add the following sentences to paragraph 3 of our sample petition:

- If you were never married before your present marriage, type this in: "Petitioner was never married before the present marriage."

- If you were previously married, type this in: "Petitioner was married prior to the present marriage in [City, County and State], on [Date] ; the marriage was terminated on [Date of final judgment] by a judgment of [Give type of termination, i.e. dissolution, divorce, nullity] at [County, State] in [Name of Court] in proceeding no. [Case Number]." If the previous marriage was terminated by death, say so.

After you finish, make at least three photocopies of the unsigned petition.

Note: Since the statements you make in the petition have not yet been accepted by the court, they are called "allegations." Even though you don't have to prove any of the allegations in order to file the petition, it's a good idea to have all your supporting documentation (listed in Chapter 2, Section D) gathered prior to filing. A common reason for delays in the adoption process is the petitioner's inability to furnish required personal documents to Social Service after filing the petition.

You file the petition by presenting the original plus three photocopies to the county clerk, either in person or by mail. (See Chapter 2, Section D on filing documents.) There is a small filing fee. You will have to pay this fee at the time you file your petition, so call ahead if you're planning to file by mail. After you file, the county clerk will return to you two or three rubber-stamped copies showing the filing date and case number.

Remember, the case number on the rubber-stamped copy of the petition is important. You will have to put the case number on all documents you file with the court.

After you file the petition, the county clerk will send a copy of it to the county Social Service Department. Everything hinges on Social Service receiving a copy of the petition, so it is important for you to satisfy yourself that Social Service has in fact received it. A week after you file your petition, call Social Service to confirm that the county clerk has sent a copy of the petition. Also ask when you should send the department copies of the personal documents you collected, which are listed in Chapter 2, Section D.

 LOS ANGELES COUNTY NOTE.
In Los Angeles, the Department of Adoptions will direct you to the county clerk to pick up a packet of forms to use during the rest of the adoption process. The packet will contain several of each form for making carbon copies. Be sure to make carbon copies—not photocopies—for these pre-printed forms.

C. The Social Services Assessment

As mentioned earlier, one of the legal requirements for adoption is that the child's best interest must be served by the adoption. It is the county Social Service Department's responsibility to make that determination.

After Social Service receives a copy of your petition, the social worker assigned to your adoption case will contact you, asking you to send certain documents if you haven't already. If you can't produce all these required documents, ask the social worker if Social Service will proceed with its assessment, getting the missing document later, or if it will delay its assessment until all documents are produced. Explain your problem frankly—the social worker may be able to help.

Social Service is required to give the court a written report with a recommendation for or against the adoption. If you, your spouse, your stepchild and the absent parent all agree to the adoption, the probabilities are that Social Service will also agree. The tendency is for the court and other government agencies to encourage, not discourage, your adoption goal. After all, the child is already living with you, so there is little to gain by opposing the adoption. Social workers tend to be much stricter about other types of adoptions, when the child is not already in the home.

You, your spouse and your stepchild will be interviewed by the social worker making the adoption assessment. You will be asked to provide some personal data and probably the names of several references.

The social worker making the assessment will not look for ways to trip you up. He will respect you for your desire to take on parental responsibility. The best approach is to deal with the worker in an honest, relaxed way. If there is something in your background that you're not proud of, be honest and bring it out if asked. Try to establish a good working relationship with the social worker. If that's not possible, it's in your interest to go out of your way to avoid creating an adversary relationship with the person making the assessment. If the facts of your situation are such that the recommendation could go either way, having the social worker emotionally on your side can make all the difference.

You may be charged a fee up to, but not exceeding, $200 for the assessment. The fee may be waived in case of economic hardship. (Family Code Section 9002.)

You will probably not get a favorable recommendation from Social Service if you have been married for less than one year. It would be best to hold off on your petition until you have been married at least a year.

Even if the report recommends against the adoption, the court must still give you a hearing. It is, however, very difficult to get a judge to approve an adoption after a negative Social Service report. You might want to withdraw your petition and forget the hearing, at least temporarily. If you still want your day in court even with a negative recommendation, you would be wise to hire a lawyer.

How long it takes Social Service to submit the adoption report to the court will depend on the caseload of the Social Service adoption unit. While county Social Service Departments have no deadline for the submittal of their reports, they try to adhere to a six-month goal. Some agencies can get the report done in a couple of months, but as caseloads increase and funding decreases, they have a tougher time—try to remember that if your social worker doesn't get to things as quickly as you'd like. You can expedite things by providing all the information or documents the agency needs. Social Service will notify you when it files the adoption report with the court, and you will receive a copy of the report.

D. GETTING THE ABSENT PARENT'S WRITTEN CONSENT

As mentioned, the absent parent must sign a formal consent in the presence of an authorized witness.[1] Usually the social worker from the county Social Service Department, in the process of making the adoption assessment, will supply the consent form, witness the signing of the consent form by the absent parent and file it with the court. Other employees of the County Social Service Department, county clerk's office or County Probation Department may also be authorized witnesses.

Ask the social worker making the assessment whether you or the department is responsible for obtaining the signed and witnessed consent of the absent parent. If you are responsible, you must take four steps:

---

[1]Your spouse and the absent parent sign consent forms independently of one another.

CONSENT FORM—PARENT IN CALIFORNIA

IN THE SUPERIOR COURT OF THE STATE OF CALIFORNIA

IN AND FOR THE COUNTY OF_____

In the Matter of the Petition of)
)   STEPPARENT ADOPTION
)
_____)   Consent to Adoption by Parent
)   in California Giving Custody
)   to Husband or Wife of Other Parent
)
)

I, the undersigned, being the father/mother of _____

_____, do hereby give my full and free consent to the

adoption of said child by _____,
                                     (Name of Petitioner)
the petitioner herein, it being fully understood by me that with the
signing of this document, my consent may not be withdrawn except with
court approval, and that with the signing of the order of adoption by
the Court, I shall give up all my rights of custody, services, and
earnings of said child, and that said child cannot be reclaimed by me.

NOTICE TO THE NATURAL PARENT WHO RELINQUISHES THE CHILD FOR ADOPTION:
"If you and your child lived together at any time as parent and child,
the adoption of your child by a stepparent does not affect the child's
right to inherit your property or the property of other blood
relatives." (Family Code § 9004)

Said child was born on _____ in _____

and is the child of _____' and _____

DATED: _____

                           _____

                                 (Signature of Parent)

SIGNED IN THE PRESENCE OF:

_____

Title

(To be witnessed by a Clerk of the Court, qualified court investigator,
a Probation Officer or by a worker at a welfare department where
stepparent investigations are delegated.) (Family Code § 9003)

1. Get a set of consent forms from the adoption unit of the Social Service Department in your county. A sample is shown on the previous page. There are two different consent forms: One for an absent parent who lives in California, and one for an absent parent who lives out-of-state.

2. See that the absent parent signs the consent forms in the presence of an authorized witness. (Generallly, it's good for the parent to sign four copies of the form; they may be needed later.)

If the absent parent lives nearby, ask the adoption worker handling your case if you can arrange for the absent parent to come to the worker's office to sign the consent.

If the absent parent lives in a different county than you do, you will have to send the consent forms to him with instructions for him to have an authorized witness watch him sign. You may have to make a few phone calls to establish just how to do this. Once the forms are signed, they should be returned to you for filing.

If the absent parent lives out-of-state, ask the Social Service Department for an out-of-state consent form. The absent parent can sign the form in front of a notary public for that state.

If the absent parent is in prison or jail, ask the social worker handling your case to send a request to the Social Service Department in the county where the prison or jail is located, asking a worker there to witness the signing of the consent. Or perhaps the administration of the prison or jail would allow the prisoner to be accompanied to the county clerk's office for the signing and witnessing.

3. File the consent forms with the county clerk. Remember—the consents should not be filed with the clerk until the petition for adoption has been filed.

4. Give a rubber-stamped copy of the consent form to the social worker.

Once a consent form is signed and witnessed, it can only be withdrawn with the approval of the court. Once the absent parent has properly executed the consent, she has no further role in the adoption and does not have to appear at the hearing.

CHILDREN BORN OUT-OF-WEDLOCK

If your stepchild was born out-of-wedlock, the natural father can give his consent without admitting paternity by signing a Denial of Paternity form. (See Section A above.) A sample is shown below.

The Denial of Paternity form is handled much like a consent form. It can be signed in the presence of a Notary Public and filed with the court like a consent form.

DENIAL OF PATERNITY

IN THE SUPERIOR COURT OF THE STATE OF CALIFORNIA

IN AND FOR THE COUNTY OF _____

In the Matter of the Adoption)
     Petition of   )
)
)   CONSENT TO ADOPTION BY
)   PARENT IN CALIFORNIA
_____)
)
)
)
)

I, the undersigned, being the father of _____

_____, do hereby give my full and free consent to the

adoption of said child by _____, the

petitioner herein, it being fully understood by me that with the
signing of this document my consent may not be withdrawn except with
court approval, and that with the signing of the order of adoption by
the court, I shall give up all my right of custody, services, and
earnings of said child, and that said child cannot be reclaimed by me.
I declare I am not the natural father of said child and am executing
the within consent to adoption solely for the purpose of promoting the
welfare and best interests of said child by facilitating said child's
adoption by petitioner.

Said child was born on _____ in _____

DATE_____, 19___. _____
                                Signature of Parent

                                _____
                                Witness of Signature of Parent

SIGNED IN THE PRESENCE OF

_____
REPRESENTATIVE: DEPARTMENT OF SOCIAL SERVICES

_____
COUNTY

(To be used when legal/natural father denies he is the natural father)

E. SCHEDULING THE ADOPTION HEARING

When the Social Service report, the consent of your spouse, and the consent of your stepchild's absent parent have all been filed with the court, you are ready to ask the Superior Court calendar clerk to schedule a court hearing on the adoption.

Usually you will not have a long wait for the hearing. Sometimes the hearing date can be set for as short a time as one week in the future, although two to four weeks is more common. If it is easier for you to appear in court on some days than on others because of job or travel commitments, make sure you explain this to the clerk. There is no reason to go to great inconvenience to show up on a particular day when the clerk could just as well schedule the hearing for another time.

When you request the hearing date, the Superior Court calendar clerk may be able to tell you the number of the room (called a Department) in which the hearing will be held. If not, you can find out on the day of the hearing (see Section G below). In some counties the department number is assigned on the morning of your hearing by the presiding judge. If this is the procedure, the calendar clerk, when he schedules the hearing, will give you the department number of the presiding judge. Before the hearing, you go to that department, where you will be given the number of the department where your hearing will be held. Sometimes the presiding judge herself hears the adoption petition.

LOS ANGELES COUNTY NOTE.
To get your hearing scheduled in Los Angeles County, you need to prepare a Memorandum for Setting for Hearing, a pre-printed form you can get from the county clerk. Put the hearing date you prefer on the Memorandum, and give an alternate date or dates. Then file it with the county clerk. You will get back a copy confirming your requested date. If the county clerk is unable to schedule the date you prefer, you will be contacted to arrive at another date.

Note on Scheduling Problems: If you have to move a considerable distance after Social Service has made its assessment, but before it submits the written report to the court, ask the county clerk if a date can be set for a special hearing without the Social Service report. If the judge will hear your petition on this basis, the actual adoption decree can be granted at a later time after the court receives the favorable adoption report from Social Service.

If you are in the military and you and your family have to move out of the area before you can get a hearing date, you may be able to appoint a person acting on your behalf to attend the hearing and sign the consent and agreement on behalf of you and your stepchild. Ask the county clerk for authorization to do this.

F. PREPARING THE ADOPTION AGREEMENT AND ADOPTION DECREE

Before the hearing, you must prepare two documents: an adoption agreement and an adoption decree. Samples are shown below. After you prepare the originals, make three copies of each unsigned form.

The adoption agreement is the document where you and your stepchild (if he is 12 or older) agree to the adoption. It is signed in the presence of the judge at the adoption hearing. You should fill it out, but not sign it, before the hearing.

LOS ANGELES COUNTY NOTE.
In Los Angeles County, you don't need to prepare an agreement. At the adoption hearing, the court will provide a "Consent and Agreement" for you to sign. You still must prepare an adoption decree, however.

The adoption decree is the court order, signed by the judge, that makes the adoption official. You prepare the decree; the judge will sign and date it at the adoption hearing.

These samples are worded as though you are a stepfather. If you are a stepmother, change the words father to mother, mother to father, wife to husband, and husband to wife. Also watch out for his, him, and her.

ADOPTION AGREEMENT

1 [YOUR NAME (In Capitals)]
   [Address]
2 [City, State, Zip]
   [Your Phone No.]
3 Petitioner In Pro Per

4

5

6

7

8   SUPERIOR COURT OF CALIFORNIA

9   COUNTY OF [Your County]

10 In the Matter of the   ) No. [Case No.]
    Adoption Petition of   )
11 [YOUR FULL NAME (In Capitals)],) ADOPTION AGREEMENT
    Adopting Parent   )
12 _____)

13   ADOPTION AGREEMENT

14   I, the undersigned petitioner, having petitioned the above

15 entitled court for the approval of the adoption of the minor child who

16 is the subject of these proceedings, do hereby agree with the State of

17 California and with the minor child that the minor child shall be

18 adopted and treated in all respects as my own lawful child should be

19 treated and that the minor child shall enjoy all the rights of a natural

20 child of my own issue, including the right of inheritance.

21   _____
                                       Petitioner
22 /////////

23 /////////

24 /////////

25 /////////

26 /////////

27 /////////

28 /////////

                              -1-

[Type in the consent for your stepchild if he/she is 12 years of age or older. If you are adopting more than one stepchild 12 or over, pluralize the consent wording and add additional signature lines.]

CONSENT OF CHILD

    I, the minor child who is the subject of these proceedings, do hereby consent to my adoption by the petitioner.

                    _____
                    [Name of stepchild]
                    Birth Certificate Name of Minor

Executed _____, 19___

In the presence of _____
                  Judge of the Superior Court

ADOPTION DECREE

```
 1   [YOUR NAME (In Capitals)]
     [Address]
 2   [City, State, Zip]
     [Your Phone No.]
 3   Petitioner In Pro Per

 4

 5

 6

 7

 8                    SUPERIOR COURT OF CALIFORNIA

 9                    COUNTY OF [Your County]

10   In the Matter of the        )   No. [Case No.]
     Adoption Petition of        )
11   [YOUR FULL NAME (In Capitals)],   )   DECREE OF ADOPTION
     Adopting Parent             )   (Stepparent)
12   _____ )

13       The petition of [Your full name] for the adoption of [Full name of

14   your stepchild], a minor, came on regularly for hearing, the petitioner

15   In Pro Per, his wife and the minor having appeared in person before the

16   court; and the court having examined each of them separately; and evi-

17   dence both real and documentary having been introduced, the court now

18   finds that:

19       All of the allegations in the petition are true; the petitioner and

20   [Full name of your wife], the natural mother, were married on [Date you

21   married your wife], and they are now husband and wife; the petitioner is

22   an adult; the minor child was born on [Birthdate of your stepchild] and

23   now resides in [Your county] County, California with the petitioner and

24   [his or her] mother.

25       All consents to the adoption required by law have been freely given

26   in the manner and form prescribed by law, and that the [Your county]

27   County Welfare Department [Substitute Probation Dept. for Welfare Dept., if appropriate,

28   or Los Angeles County Department of Adoptions if yours is an L.A. Petition] has filed with
```

-1-

1   the court its report and recommendation that the petition be granted.

2   The petitioner has executed in the presence of the court an agree-

3   ment that the child shall be adopted and treated in all respects as the

4   petitioner's own lawful child.

5   The best interests and welfare of the child will be promoted by the

6   proposed adoption. The child is a proper subject for adoption, and the

7   petitioner's home is suitable for the child. The court further finds

8   that the petition should be granted.

9   IT IS THEREFORE ORDERED that the minor child is now the adopted

10   child of the petitioner and that the petitioner and the child shall

11   hereafter sustain toward each other the legal relation of parent and

12   child subject to all the rights and duties of that relationship, includ-

13   ing all legal rights and duties of custody, support, and inheritance and

14   that the child shall hereafter be known as [New full name of your step-

15   child. If your stepchild's name is not being changed, place a period after the word "inheri-

16   tance," and leave out the rest of the sentence.].

17

18   Dated: _____

19   _____

20   Judge of the Superior Court

21

22

23

24

25

26

27

28

-2-

G. THE ADOPTION HEARING

The big day has arrived. You and your stepchild have a date with the judge. Relax—it will be lots easier than you think. A judge has to deal with hostile, scared people all day. It will be a pleasure for her to take a few minutes to help some nice people get their family on solid legal footing.

Adoption hearings do not take place in open court. They are usually held in the judge's private office, and no unauthorized persons are admitted. You and your stepchild are required to appear at the hearing. It's usual for your spouse to also appear, but this is not technically required as long as his signed consent is on file.

EMERGENCIES

If, at the last minute, illness or an emergency prevents you or your stepchild from attending the hearing, immediately phone the Clerk of the Superior Court to explain and request that the hearing be rescheduled. This will not be difficult to arrange.

When you go to the hearing, take the adoption decree and the adoption agreement, plus the photocopies. It's a good idea to take your rubber-stamped copy of the adoption petition and copies of the other documents you've filed, even though the judge should have the originals in the court file. Also, take copies of the personal documents you gathered (see Section B above).

Leave home early so you will arrive at the courthouse in plenty of time to do some scouting around for the right room (department). If you weren't given the department number ahead of time, ask for the department number at the clerk's office. In some courthouses, department assignments are posted on bulletin boards in the lobby each morning. You may wish to check there before asking the clerk.

Once you are sure that you are in the correct department, sit and wait until the judge is ready for you. If you arrive before the court starts, identify yourself to the judge's clerk, who will be bustling around the courtroom a few minutes before the judge appears.

The actual adoption hearing will be very short. The judge will rely primarily on the Social Service report and may or may not ask you a few questions. It is normal for the judge to read you the adoption agreement and ask if you agree. After the judge indicates that the adoption petition should be granted, you sign the adoption agreement, and if your stepchild is 12 years of age or older, she signs a consent statement. The judge signs the adoption decree. The whole hearing usually lasts less than five minutes, which includes time for handshakes and smiles all around.

H. AFTER THE HEARING

You still have a few loose ends to tie up after the hearing is over.

1. Filing the Decree

After the hearing, you must take the originals and copies of the adoption decree and the adoption agreement to the county clerk for filing. It's a good time to have one or more rubber-stamped copies of the decree certified if you do not plan on amending the birth certificate. It will give you authenticated proof of the adoption just in case you ever need it. If you prefer some form of official proof of the adoption other than the adoption decree, ask the county clerk if you can have an "Adoption Certificate." Some counties issue this certificate and some do not. It is not legally necessary, but it is nice to have it available.

2. Getting the Birth Certificate Amended

The form used by the state to amend the birth certificate is the Court Report of Adoption form. After the adoption decree is filed, the county clerk must send it to the California Registrar of Vital Statistics. This form contains information and statistics on you, your spouse and your newly adopted child. Depending on your county's policy, the Social Service Department may enter the information on the form and file it with the court before the adoption hearing, or the county clerk may enter the information at the time you file the adoption decree. In either event, you will be required to verify the information at the time you file the decree.

COURT REPORT OF ADOPTION

STATE BIRTH CERTIFICATE NUMBER

LOCAL REGISTRATION DISTRICT AND CERTIFICATE NUMBER

PART I   The information in this section must be given as it was before adoption. Without this data it may be impossible to prepare an amended certificate of birth for this child.

COMPLETE THIS FORM IN BLACK INK.

FACTS OF BIRTH

1A. NAME OF CHILD—FIRST NAME	1B. MIDDLE NAME	1C. LAST NAME

2. SEX	3. DATE OF BIRTH	4. NAME OF PHYSICIAN OR OTHER PERSON WHO ATTENDED THIS BIRTH

5A. PLACE OF BIRTH—NAME OF HOSPITAL	5B. CITY OR TOWN	5C. STATE OR FOREIGN COUNTRY

NATURAL PARENTS' DATA

6A. NAME OF FATHER—FIRST NAME	6B. MIDDLE NAME	6C. LAST NAME

7A. BIRTH NAME OF MOTHER—FIRST NAME	7B. MIDDLE NAME	7C. LAST NAME (BIRTH SURNAME)

PART II   Adopting parents must furnish the following information concerning themselves as it was at the date of birth of the above child. This information is used in preparation of the amended certificate of birth.

CHECK APPROPRIATE BOX
ADOPTIVE ☐
OR
NATURAL ☐
FATHER

8A. NAME OF FATHER—FIRST NAME	8B. MIDDLE NAME	8C. LAST NAME (BIRTH SURNAME)

9. BIRTHPLACE (STATE OR FOREIGN COUNTRY)	10. DATE OF BIRTH OF FATHER (ENTER MONTH, DAY, YEAR)

CHECK APPROPRIATE BOX
ADOPTIVE ☐
OR
NATURAL ☐
MOTHER

11A. BIRTH NAME OF MOTHER—FIRST NAME	11A. MIDDLE NAME	11C. LAST NAME (BIRTH SURNAME)

12. BIRTHPLACE (STATE OR FOREIGN COUNTRY)	13. DATE OF BIRTH OF MOTHER (ENTER MONTH, DAY, YEAR)

INSTRUCTIONS TO STATE REGISTRAR

14. DO YOU WANT AN AMENDED BIRTH RECORD PREPARED?	(SPECIFY YES OR NO)	15. DO YOU WANT THE NAME OF THE HOSPITAL OR OTHER FACILITY WHERE BIRTH OCCURRED OMITTED, AS PROVIDED IN SECTION 10433 OF THE HEALTH AND SAFETY CODE?	(SPECIFY YES OR NO)	16. WHEN A CHILD IS ADOPTED BY AN UNMARRIED MAN OR WOMAN, SPECIFY IF THE PARENT REQUESTS THAT THE AMENDED CERTIFICATE REFLECT THE FACT THAT THE ADOPTION WAS A SINGLE PARENT ADOPTION, AS PROVIDED FOR IN SECTION 10433.1 OF THE HEALTH AND SAFETY CODE?	(SPECIFY YES OR NO)

VERIFICATION OF PART II

17. SIGNATURE AND MAILING ADDRESS OF PARENT VERIFYING DATA IN PART II
▶

AGENCY OR DEPARTMENT

18. NAME AND MAILING ADDRESS OF AGENCY OR DEPARTMENT WHICH INVESTIGATED OR HANDLED CASE

ATTORNEY

19. NAME AND MAILING ADDRESS OF ATTORNEY

PART III   The county clerk should require that as much of the information as is available in Parts I and II, above, be furnished before he completes Part III and forwards the report to the State Registrar of Vital Statistics.

COUNTY CLERK

20. I HEREBY CERTIFY THAT THE CHILD DESCRIBED ABOVE WAS ADOPTED BY THE ABOVE NAMED ADOPTIVE PARENT(S) ON THE _____ DAY OF _____ 19 ___ AS SET FORTH IN THE DECREE OF ADOPTION MADE ON THAT DATE. IN CASE NUMBER _____	21. DATE OF FILING OF PETITION
	22. THE NAME OF THE CHILD AS SET FORTH IN THE DECREE OF ADOPTION

23. SIGNATURE AND SEAL OF COUNTY CLERK ▶	BY:	24. DATE SIGNED	25. CLERK IN AND FOR THE COUNTY OF

NAME AND MAILING ADDRESS OF PERSON TO WHOM CERTIFIED COPY IS TO BE SENT

NAME
STREET ADDRESS
ADDRESS—CITY OR TOWN, STATE, ZIP CODE

STATE OF CALIFORNIA, DEPARTMENT OF HEALTH SERVICES, OFFICE OF THE STATE REGISTRAR OF VITAL STATISTICS

VS-44 (9-82)

If you don't want the certificate amended, indicate this on the form. If you request a birth certificate amendment, the state will mail you a certified copy of the amended certificate. This takes several weeks.

If your stepchild was born in a state other than California, the California Registrar of Vital Statistics will forward the Court Report of Adoption to the appropriate agency of the other state. The California Registrar will then send you a notice advising you to write that agency to find out how to apply for an amended birth certificate.

3. Time to Relax

It's over! You have done your own adoption and probably saved at least $700 in attorney fees. Congratulations! If your stepchild is older, she has probably watched you typing and shuffling paperwork and has gotten to participate. She has calmly watched as you sat before the judge, shifting a little nervously in your chair. She has watched with interest as one of the clerks stamped your documents after the hearing. To your adopted child, the whole thing was probably more interesting than a trip to the zoo. If she is too young to realize what was happening, some day you might want to relive the process. In any event, now you can add the adoption decree to your file of papers marked "Important Documents," put your typewriter away for a while and have a little family celebration. Above all, you can relax.

You and your family may find it helpful to talk to a counselor who has experience with "blended families." For a referral, call your county mental health agency.

I.   CHECKLIST: WHEN THE ABSENT PARENT CONSENTS TO THE ADOPTION

Here is a checklist with the important steps in the adoption process.

Note: If you are filing in Los Angeles County, see Section J below instead of this section.

1. _____ Gather documentation listed in Chapter 2, Section D.

2. _____ Prepare the adoption petition. (Section B)

3. _____ File the petition by presenting the original plus three photocopies to the county clerk and paying the modest fee. The county clerk will return to you either two or three rubber-stamped copies of the petition with the case number and the filing date. (Section B)

4. _____ Call the adoption unit of the county Social Service Department and verify that it has received a copy of your adoption petition from the county clerk. (Section B)

5. _____ Cooperate with the adoption worker who makes the adoption assessment. (Section C) Work with him in making arrangements for the absent parent to sign the consent. If Social Service tells you that it is your responsibility to see that the absent parent has his signature on the consent form properly witnessed, do the following (Section D):

    a. Get four copies of the consent form from the Social Service Department.

    b. Type in the forms.

    c. Have the absent parent sign the consent forms in the presence of a Social Service employee or other authorized witness.

    d. File the signed consent forms with the county clerk and give a rubber-stamped copy to the adoption worker.

6. _____ After Social Service submits its adoption report to the court (you will be notified), contact the Superior Court calendar clerk at the county clerk's office. Request a hearing date convenient to you. (Section E)

7. _____ Prepare an (unsigned) original and three photocopies of each of these documents (Section F):

- Adoption decree.

- Adoption agreement (including consent statement for your step-child if she is 12 or older).

8. _____ Attend the adoption hearing with your spouse and your stepchild, bringing the forms and photocopies you prepared in the above step. Also bring the documents you gathered in Step 1 and your rubber-stamped photocopy of the adoption petition. (Section G)

9. _____ After the hearing, file the adoption decree and the adoption agreement with the county clerk. Take back your rubber-stamped photocopies and have at least one copy of the adoption decree certified. (Section H)

10. _____ On the Court Report of Adoption form, verify information and indicate whether or not you want your stepchild's original birth certificate amended. (Section H)

FORMS LIST FOR ADOPTION WHEN ABSENT PARENT CONSENTS

Petition for Adoption
Adoption Decree
Adoption Agreement (includes stepchild's consent)

J. CHECKLIST FOR LOS ANGELES COUNTY

Los Angeles County procedure has some differences, although most of the steps in an adoption proceeding are the same as in other counties. Here is a checklist.

1. _____ Gather documentation listed in Chapter 2, Section D.

2. _____ Prepare the adoption petition. Make three photocopies. (Section B)

3. _____ File the adoption petition by presenting the original and photocopies to the county clerk. The county clerk will return three photocopies of the petition, rubber-stamped with the case number and filing date. (Section B)

4. _____ Call the Los Angeles County Department of Adoptions to verify that it has received a copy of your petition from the county clerk. (Section B)

5. _____ Cooperate with the adoption worker who makes the adoption assessment. Work with him in making arrangements for the absent parent to sign the consent. (Section C)

6. _____ After you are notified that the adoption report has been filed, prepare and file a Memorandum for Setting for Hearing. (Section E)

7. _____ Before the adoption hearing, prepare an original and three photocopies of the adoption decree. (Section F)

8. _____ Attend the adoption hearing with your spouse and your stepchild, and bring the adoption decree. At the hearing, the court will furnish an adoption agreement (referred to as Consent and Agreement) for you (and your stepchild, if 12 or older) to sign. (Section G)

9. _____ After the hearing you will either be given your rubber-stamped copies of the adoption decree or they will be mailed to you. Ask the county clerk to certify at least one of your rubber-stamped copies. On the Court Report of Adoption form, verify information and indicate whether or not you want your stepchild's original birth certificate amended. (Section H)

Chapter 5

ADOPTION BASED ON PARENT'S FAILURE TO SUPPORT CHILD

If the missing parent has willfully failed to meet his parental responsibilities—that is, if he has failed to support and communicate with the child (see Chapter 3, Section B)—you can file an adoption petition following the procedures in this chapter.

Because all stepparent adoptions, regardless of the grounds on which they are based, follow basically the same procedure, this chapter sometimes refers you to Chapter 4 (Adoption If the Absent Parent Consents), instead of repeating discussions of procedural steps covered there.

Reminder: You can also base an adoption petition on the parent's "abandonment" of the child—that is, his failure to support the child **or** failure to communicate with the child for a year or more. See Chapter 3 for how to choose the best procedure for your situation.

A. HOW TO START: THE ADOPTION PETITION

In an adoption petition based on the parent's willful failure to support and communicate with the child, you allege the "willful failure" by the missing parent, and you ask the court to require only the consent of your spouse for the adoption.

PETITION FOR ADOPTION

```
 1   [YOUR NAME (In Capitals)]
     [Address]
 2   [City, State Zip]
     [Your Phone No.]
 3   Petitioner In Pro Per

 4

 5

 6

 7

 8                    SUPERIOR COURT OF CALIFORNIA

 9                    COUNTY OF [Your County]

10   In the Matter of the        )  No.[Case No.]
     Adoption Petition of        )
11   [YOUR FULL NAME (In Capitals)],  )  PETITION FOR ADOPTION
     Adopting Parent             )  (Stepparent)
12   _____)

13        [YOUR FULL NAME], Petitioner, alleges:

14        1. The name by which the minor who is the subject of this petition

15   was registered at birth is [Full name of your stepchild as it appears on

16   birth certificate].[If the child's name was changed after birth, add: Thereafter, the

17   child's name was changed to [Changed name] pursuant to [Court, order

18   number, date.]

19        2. The minor child is a [male or female] born on [Birthdate] in

20   [City and State of birth]. [If your stepchild is 12 or over, add: [He/She] is pre-

21   pared to consent to [his/her] adoption by Petitioner.]

22        3. Petitioner is an adult person and desires to adopt the minor

23   child. Petitioner is the husband of [Full name of your wife], who is the

24   mother of the child and who has custody of the child. Petitioner, his

25   spouse and the child reside in [Your County] County, California. [See Los

26   Angeles County Note at end of petition.]

27        4. The natural mother and father of the minor were married in [City

28   and State] on [Date]; the marriage was terminated on [Final Judgment of
```

-1-

1 Dissolution Date] in [Name of Court] in proceeding No. [Case No.]. For

2 more than one year last past, the father has failed to communicate with

3 and to pay for the care, support and education of the minor when able to

4 do so.

5   5. The mother of the child, [Full name of your wife], was married

6 to Petitioner on [Date you and your wife were married] at [City and

7 state] and is prepared to consent to the minor's adoption by Petitioner,

8 retaining all her rights of custody and control.

9   6. The child is a proper subject for adoption, and Petitioner is

10 willing and able to care for the child properly. The child's best inter-

11 ests will be promoted by this adoption. Petitioner agrees to adopt the

12 child and treat the child in all respects as his own lawful child.

13   WHEREFORE, Petitioner prays that the Court grant this petition and

14 decree that the child has been legally adopted by Petitioner, and that

15 Petitioner and child shall thenceforth sustain toward each other the

16 legal relation of parent and child and with all rights and duties of

17 that relation, and that the child shall be known as [New name]. [If your

18 stepchild's name is not being changed, end the sentence after the word "relation."]

19   [Your signature]_____
                                      Petitioner
20

21   VERIFICATION

22   The statements in the above Petition are true of my own knowledge,

23 except as to the matters that are therein stated on my information and

24 belief, and as to those matters I believe them to be true.

25   Executed on _____, 19__, at _____, California.

26   I declare under penalty of perjury that the foregoing is true and

27 correct.

28   [Your signature]_____
                                      Petitioner

                                    -2-

LOS ANGELES COUNTY NOTE.
In Los Angeles County, the petitioner must include information in the adoption petition on his previous marriage(s). Add the following to paragraph 3:

- If you (the petitioner) were never married previously, "Petitioner was never married prior to the present marriage."

- If you were previously married, "Petitioner was married prior to the present marriage in [City and State] on [Date]; the marriage was terminated on [Date of Final Judgment] by a judgment of [Give type of termination, e.g., dissolution, divorce, nullity] at [County, State] in [Name of Court] in proceeding no. [Case No.]." If the previous marriage was terminated by death, say so.

The petition shown above is worded as though you are a stepfather. If you are a stepmother, change the words father to mother, mother to father, wife to husband and husband to wife. Also watch out for his, him and her.

After you prepare the petition, make three photocopies. You file the petition by presenting the original plus three photocopies to the county clerk, either in person or by mail. (See Chapter 2, Section D on filing documents.) There is no actual filing fee, but there is a small fee for processing by the state. You will have to pay this fee at the time you file your petition, so call ahead if you're planning to file by mail. After you file, the county clerk will return to you two or three rubber-stamped copies showing the filing date and case number.

After you file the adoption petition, wait about a week and then call the Social Service Department (in Los Angeles County, the Department of Adoptions) to make sure it has received a copy of your petition from the county clerk.

LOS ANGELES COUNTY NOTE.
The Department of Adoptions will direct you to the county clerk to pick up a packet of forms to use during the rest of the adoption process. The packet will contain several of each form.

B. THE SOCIAL SERVICE ASSESSMENT

Before the court will hold a hearing to rule on the adoption petition, the County Social Service Department must make an adoption assessment and submit its written report and recommendation to the court. The adoption cannot be ordered by the judge unless the social service agency gives its approval.[1]

The evaluation process is discussed in Chapter 4, Section C. The Social Service Department does not concern itself with attempting to prove or disprove your allegation of "willful failure." The welfare of your stepchild is its main concern. If

---

[1] When the other parent gives his consent to the adoption (Chapter 4), social service approval is not required, although the agency's recommendation is given considerable weight by the judge.

Social Service believes the adoption will be beneficial for the child, you will get a positive recommendation.

C. NOTIFYING THE ABSENT PARENT

It stands to reason that the absent parent has a legal right to know about your attempt to adopt his child. So before you can have a hearing on the adoption, you must give (or at least try to give) the absent parent a copy of your adoption petition and a citation telling him to appear at the upcoming hearing.

- If you know where the absent parent lives or works, you must try to have someone give him a notice personally. That process is called "serving" the notice and is discussed in this section.
- If you don't know the whereabouts of the absent parent, skip to Section D for instructions on how to give legally sufficient notice.

1. Who Can Serve the Papers?

The notice must be served by someone who is at least 18 years of age and not a party to the action. This means neither you nor your spouse can do it yourself, because you are parties. The person making service can be a professional process server or a sheriff, marshal or constable. If service can be made inside California, you can have a friend or relative do it for you. Out of state, use a professional. Whoever serves the papers for you must fill out a Proof of Service form, to prove to the court that the notice was served properly.

2. The Papers to Be Served

You must serve the parent with a copy (not the original) of a citation (Citation to Appear) ordering him to appear in court, together with a file-endorsed copy of the adoption petition. The original citation is kept by the server and returned to you for filing with a Proof of Service form filled out. Instructions for preparing the citation are in Section D3 below.

3. Choosing the Method of Service

There are several different ways papers can be served on the absent parent. Each of them is discussed below.

If the absent parent is in California, you have three options:

   a. Personal service;

   b. Service by mail and acknowledgment; or

c. Substituted service (service on someone else if the parent can't be served).

If the parent is outside of California, you have these three choices:

a. Personal service;

b. Service by mail and acknowledgment; or

c. Certified mail, return receipt requested.

If the parent will be cooperative, then service by mail and acknowledgment is easiest. If the parent is out of state and will not try to avoid receiving a certified letter, then service by certified mail is best. If you know where the parent is located, but aren't sure how cooperative he will be, then personal service is surest. If in doubt, try one of the easier methods first. If none of these methods works, you will have to resort to publishing the notice in a newspaper (Section D below).

a. Personal Service

If you can find the parent, you can have papers served personally. This means that the server must personally hand the parent the papers to be served. Whoever is going to serve the papers must be given the following items:

1. A photo or description of the person to be served, if possible.

2. The best and most complete information about where the person can be found, at home and at work.

3. The original and one copy of the citation. If service is to be made out-of-state, send the server only a copy, not the original citation.

4. A file-endorsed copy of the adoption petition.

If you decide to use a county sheriff, marshal or constable, call ahead to check procedures. You will probably be able to just mail these items to the office of one of those officials nearest the parent and request service, with a money order for the fee.

If you decide to have a friend or relative make service, all he needs to do is hand the papers to the parent. If the parent may be a bit sticky about being served, the process server should know that once the person has been located and identified, the server should say, "I have court papers for you." If the parent won't open the door, turns and runs, or in any other way tries to avoid service, the server can just drop the papers and leave, and service will have been effectively completed.

After service, make sure that the server fills out the Proof of Service properly. If personal service is made outside California, it must be proved by a sworn and notarized affidavit; for this reason, use only a professional server or an official and request that he send his affidavit of service to you. Attach this to the Proof of Service when you file it.

ACKNOWLEDGMENT

<table>
<tr>
<td colspan="2">NAME AND ADDRESS OF SENDER   TELEPHONE NO.</td>
<td>FOR COURT USE ONLY</td>
</tr>
<tr>
<td colspan="2">Insert name of court judicial district or branch court if any and Post Office and Street Address</td>
<td></td>
</tr>
<tr>
<td colspan="2">PLAINTIFF</td>
<td></td>
</tr>
<tr>
<td colspan="2">DEFENDANT</td>
<td></td>
</tr>
<tr>
<td>NOTICE AND ACKNOWLEDGMENT OF RECEIPT</td>
<td colspan="2">Case Number</td>
</tr>
</table>

TO: ....
(insert name of individual being served)

    This summons and other document(s) indicated below are being served pursuant to Section 415.30 of the California Code of Civil Procedure. Your failure to complete this form and return it to me within 20 days may subject you (or the party on whose behalf you are being served) to liability for the payment of any expenses incurred in serving a summons on you in any other manner permitted by law.

    If you are being served on behalf of a corporation, unincorporated association (including a partnership), or other entity, this form must be signed by you in the name of such entity or by a person authorized to receive service of process on behalf of such entity. In all other cases, this form must be signed by you personally or by a person authorized by you to acknowledge receipt of summons. Section 415.30 provides that this summons and other document(s) are deemed served on the date you sign the Acknowledgment of Receipt below, if you return this form to me.

Dated: _____
                                                    (Signature of sender)

ACKNOWLEDGMENT OF RECEIPT

This acknowledges receipt of (To be completed by sender before mailing)
1. ☐   A copy of the summons and of the complaint.
2. ☐   A copy of the summons and of the Petition (Marriage) and :
    ☐   Blank Confidential Counseling Statement (Marriage)
    ☐   Order to Show Cause (Marriage)
    ☐   Blank Responsive Declaration
    ☐   Blank Financial Declaration
    ☐   Other (Specify)

(To be completed by recipient)

Date of receipt: ....   _____
                                          (Signature of person acknowledging receipt, with title if
                                          acknowledgment is made on behalf of another person)

Date this form is signed : ....   _____
                                          (Type or print your name and name of entity,
                                          if any, on whose behalf this form is signed)

5   Form Approved by the
Judicial Council of California   **NOTICE AND ACKNOWLEDGMENT OF RECEIPT**   CCP 415.30, 417.10;
Revised Effective January 1, 1975   Cal. Rules of Court,
                                             Rule 1216
76N629R—8-77—PS 10-77
RC031

b. Service By Mail and Acknowledgment

If you know the parent's address, and if he will cooperate to the extent of signing an Acknowledgment, then your job is easy. A copy of the citation and adoption petition should be mailed by first class mail, postage prepaid, to the parent, together with the original and one copy of the Acknowledgment and a return envelope, postage prepaid, addressed to the sender. Remember, someone other than yourself (or your spouse) who is at least 18 years old must do the mailing for you. Service is complete when the parent signs the Acknowledgment.

When the parent receives the papers, he only needs to enter the date he received them, sign the original Acknowledgment and return it to the sender. The sender then completes the Proof of Service, attaches the original Acknowledgment, and the job is complete. Service by this method is effective on the date the Acknowledgment is signed by the person served.

c. Substituted Service

Your server may also leave a copy of the notice at the parent's office, or, after making unsuccessful attempts at personal service, at the person's home. The notice must be left with someone "apparently in charge" of the office or with a "competent member of the household," at least 18 years old, at the parent's home.

After a copy is left with someone in this manner, the server must mail (first-class mail is sufficient) another copy of the notice to the place the first copy was left. Service is deemed complete ten days after the date of mailing.

d. Service by Certified or Registered Mail— Outside California Only

When you know the parent's address outside California, you can serve papers on him by having someone over 18 mail the papers via registered or certified mail, with a return receipt requested. Make sure you indicate "deliver to addressee only" on the post office form. When the return receipt comes back with the parent's signature, it must be filed as a part of the Proof of Service.

When using this method, the service is deemed completed on the 10th day after mailing. Use that date as the date of service.

Note: If the parent won't sign for the mail, you will have to serve him by personal service.

4. The Proof of Service

This is a sworn statement that proves to the court that the required steps were actually carried out to serve the notice on the parent. The server fills out the proof of service, and you file it and the original citation with the county clerk as soon as service is effective. If you lose or misplace the original citation you will need to prepare an affidavit of "Lost Summons."

How to Fill Out the Proof of Service

Caption: Have the server type your name and address, the name of the court, and the case number in the boxes at the top of the form. For "short title," put "Adoption Petition of [Your Name]."

Item 1: Type in "Citation to Appear."

Item 2: a. Type the name of the parent served.

b. Check the first box unless substituted service was made, in which case you should check the "other" box and type in the name of the person to whom the citation was given.

c. Type in the address of the person served.

Item 3: Check box a (personal service), b (substituted service), or c (mailing), whichever is appropriate, and type in the date and time of service.

If box b is checked, also check the "business" or "home" box and check box (5). The server will need to attach a short statement, titled "Declaration of Diligence" and made under penalty of perjury, setting out his attempts to make personal service before he resorted to substituted service.

If box c is checked, also check either box (3) or (4). Remember to attach the return receipt or signed acknowledgment.

Box e should be checked only if the citation was published in a newspaper. If the server checks it, he should type in "publication, C.C.P. sec. 415.50. "

Item 4: Check box a. (True, the missing parent isn't really a "defendant," but this is a general form, not designed just for adoptions, and that's the closest it comes to your situation.)

Item 5: Here the server types in his name, address and phone number. If he charged a fee for serving the citation, he should enter that in 5.a. He should also check either box b or d.

Item 6: Check this box.

Reminder: If service was made outside California, attach the professional server's affidavit of service.

The server should sign and date the proof of service. The original should be attached to the orignal citation and filed. Make a copy for your records.

ATTORNEY OR PARTY WITHOUT ATTORNEY *(Name and Address)*:		TELEPHONE NO.:	FOR COURT USE ONLY
		Ref. No. or File No.	
ATTORNEY FOR *(Name)*:			
Insert name of court and name of judicial district and branch court, if any:			
SHORT TITLE OF CASE:			

PROOF OF SERVICE (Summons)	DATE:	TIME:	DEPT./DIV.:	CASE NUMBER:

1. At the time of service I was at least 18 years of age and not a party to this action, and **I served copies** of the *(specify documents)*:

2. a. Party served *(specify name of party as shown on the documents served)*:

   b. Person served: ☐ party in item 2a ☐ other *(specify name and title or relationship to the party named in item 2a)*:

   c. Address:

3. I served the party named in item 2
   a. ☐ **by personally delivering** the copies   (1) on *(date)*:   (2) at *(time)*:
   b. ☐ **by leaving** the copies with or in the presence of *(name and title or relationship to person indicated in item 2b)*:

      (1) ☐ **(business)** a person at least 18 years of age apparently in charge at the office or usual place of business of the person served. I informed him or her of the general nature of the papers.
      (2) ☐ **(home)** a competent member of the household (at least 18 years of age) at the dwelling house or usual place of abode of the person served. I informed him or her of the general nature of the papers.
      (3) on *(date)*:   (4) at *(time)*:
      (5) ☐ A **declaration of diligence** is attached. *(Substituted service on natural person, minor, conservatee, or candidate.)*
   c. ☐ **by mailing** the copies to the person served, addressed as shown in item 2c, by first-class mail, postage prepaid,
      (1) on *(date)*:   (2) from *(city)*:
      (3) ☐ with two copies of the Notice and Acknowledgment of Receipt and a postage-paid return envelope addressed to me.
      (4) ☐ to an address outside California with return receipt requested.   ◀ *(Attach completed form.)* ✈
   d. ☐ **by causing** copies to be mailed. A declaration of mailing is attached.
   e. ☐ **other** *(specify other manner of service and authorizing code section)*:

4. The "Notice to the Person Served" (on the summons) was completed as follows:
   a. ☐ as an individual defendant.
   b. ☐ as the person sued under the fictitious name of *(specify)*:
   c. ☐ on behalf of *(specify)*:
      under: ☐ CCP 416.10 (corporation)   ☐ CCP 416.60 (minor)   ☐ other:
             ☐ CCP 416.20 (defunct corporation)   ☐ CCP 416.70 (conservatee)
             ☐ CCP 416.40 (association or partnership) ☐ CCP 416.90 (individual)

5. **Person serving** *(name, address, and telephone No.)*:
   a. **Fee** for service: $
   b. ☐ Not a registered California process server.
   c. ☐ Exempt from registration under B&P § 22350(b).
   d. ☐ Registered California process server.
      (1) ☐ Employee or independent contractor.
      (2) Registration No.:
      (3) County:

6. ☐ I declare under penalty of perjury under the laws of the State of California that the foregoing is true and correct.
7. ☐ I am a **California sheriff, marshal, or constable** and I certify that the foregoing is true and correct.

Date: _____   ▶ _____
                                              (SIGNATURE)

Form Adopted by Rule 982 Judicial Council of California 982(a)(23) [New July 1, 1987]	**PROOF OF SERVICE** (Summons)	Code Civ. Proc., § 417.10(f)

D. PUBLISHING NOTICE TO THE MISSING PARENT

As mentioned above, if you can't find the missing parent you must still try to give him notice of the adoption. The law allows you to meet this requirement by publishing a legal notice (citation) in a newspaper, ordering the missing parent to appear at the adoption hearing.

Publishing the citation requires these steps:

1. Making a concerted effort to find the parent.

2. Asking the court to authorize the publication.

3. Demonstrating to the court your efforts to find the parent.

4. Getting a signed order from a judge authorizing you to publish.

5. Getting the notice (citation) approved by the county clerk.

6. Setting the hearing date.

7. Publishing the citation in an approved newspaper at least once a week for four successive weeks.

8. Proving to the court that the citation was published.

When can you start the publication process? Because the point of publication is to tell the absent parent about the hearing, you can't publish until a hearing date has been set. Thus the answer depends on your county's policy on when a hearing date may be placed on the court calendar. In most counties, the county clerk cannot set a hearing date until Social Service files its report on the adoption. Thus, you must wait for the report to be filed (or determine from the agency that it will soon be filed) before beginning the search. Otherwise, you might conduct the search and then, by the time the report is filed, your search might not be considered current enough to justify publication of the citation. Here is how the process looks:

1. Petition filed.

2. Agency report filed (or agency confirms that the report will be filed within approximately 90 days).

3. Search for missing parent made.

4. Order for Publication obtained, hearing date set, citation issued (all at essentially the same time).

5. Publication.

6. Adoption hearing.

Check with your county clerk and the Social Service worker who's assigned to your case to determine exactly how your county conducts this procedure.

 LOS ANGELES COUNTY NOTE.
In Los Angeles County, the hearing date is normally set before the adoption report is filed by Social Service. This means that you can start the publication process immediately after filing the petition. Here are the steps, in order:

1. Petition filed.

2. Search for missing parent made.

3. Order for Publication obtained, hearing date set, citation issued.

4. Publication.

5. Agency report filed.

6. Adoption hearing.

1. Try to Find the Absent Parent

Before a court will allow you to notify the missing parent of the hearing by publication, you must show that you can't find the parent to notify him personally.[2]

When you try to find the missing parent, keep records of your activities, entering the date of each attempt. If someone else conducts the search, the person making the inquiry should sign a declaration or affidavit setting out her attempts and findings. The declarations must be attached to the application when you ask the court to order publication (section 3 below). If inquiry is made by mail, returned correspondence or evidence of mailing must be attached.

The following search techniques are taken from the search criteria issued by the Los Angeles County Superior Court. Generally speaking, you will need to follow these steps before a court will allow you to notify the absent parent by publication.

a. Find the last known address of the missing parent. You will have to tell the court how, when and from whom you obtained the address.

b. Make inquiries (keep track of the dates) at the last known address. If the people living at the missing parent's last known address have no information on his whereabouts, ask the neighbors on the right and left. This can be done either by letter or by sending an investigator to the neighborhood.

If the last known address is a mental or a penal institution, contact the person in charge of the institution, ask for current information from its records, and then contact that address.

---

[2]If you do know the address of the absent parent but are publishing notice because you can't make service in any of the ways discussed in Section C above, you can skip this step.

c. Make inquiries of all known relatives, friends, employers, and other persons likely to know the whereabouts of the missing parent. You must tell the court their names and what relationship they are to the parent. Give dates and results of your inquiries, e.g., "There are no known relatives, friends, employers, or other persons likely to know the whereabouts of the citee," or "The only person(s) likely to know the whereabouts of citee is [give name(s) and relationship(s) to citee]."

d. Check with your county clerk to see if your county requires that you contact the military services. Your court may require that you present certificates, at or before the adoption hearing, from the five military services showing that central personnel records show that the missing parent is not on active duty with the military. If after checking with the county clerk, there is any doubt in your mind regarding whether or not the court requires the certificates, go ahead and send for them to avoid the possibility of the judge refusing to approve your petition at the hearing.

ADDRESSES OF THE MILITARY SERVICES

Army	Personnel Records Branch, Personnel Division Office of the Adjutant General Department of the Army Washington 20025, D.C.
Navy	Chief of Naval Personnel Attn: Perse-2 and E 0 3 Department of the Navy Washington 20025, D.C.
Air Force	Director, Administrative Services Attn: Military Personnel Records Service Headquarters United States Air Force Washington 20025, D.C.
Coast Guard	The Commandant U.S. Coast Guard Washington 20025, D.C.
Marines	Data Processing Section - Code D G K Headquarters United States Marine Corps Washington 20025, D.C.

Your letter to each military service might go something like this:

February 3, 19__

Re: John James Smith

Born: Dec. 2, 1950
Birthplace: Anywhere, Calif.
Social Security No. 123-45-6789
Race: Caucasian
Height: 5'10"
Prior Military Service: None

Sir:

I am requesting from you a certificate showing that you
have searched your personnel files to determine if John James
Smith is on active duty in your branch of the military
service.
I am in need of this information in connection with my
petition to adopt the natural child of Mr. Smith. Enclosed is
a money order for $15.00 and a self-addressed stamped
envelope. Please return any amount in excess of your actual
fee.

Since my stepchild's adoption depends upon receipt of the
requested certificate, your fastest attention to this
request would be greatly appreciated by my stepchild and
myself.

Very truly yours,

Paul Victor Hart

LOS ANGELES COUNTY NOTE.
If the absent parent has ever resided in Los Angeles County, then a local search is required. A legal news paper (look in the yellow pages for names and numbers) will make such a search and document it on a "Declaration of Search" form it will give you. You must make inquiries at the addresses and telephone numbers given on the Declaration of Search. Keep track of the dates and results of such inquiries. Attach the Declaration of Search to the Application for Publication (Section 3 below). If the citee has never resided in the County of Los Angeles, state in your application that "a declaration of search is not required because the citee has never resided in the County of Los Angeles."

e. Contact the Department of Motor Vehicles. Although drivers are now allowed by law to keep the DMV from giving out their addresses, a report from the Department of Motor Vehicles is required if the missing parent ever resided in California. Write and ask for the current address from the Department of Motor Vehicles, Division of Driver's Licenses, P.O. Box 2590, Sacramento, California 95812. There is a fee for this information, so ask the DMV before you write. Send your inquiry to Motor Vehicles early in your search; if you don't get the reply within about 90 days, your search may be considered obsolete when you ask the court to order publication. Recent inquiries must be made to addresses given by the DMV. Again, keep records of the dates and results of such inquiries.

f. Contact the Registrar of Voters and County Tax Assessor in the county of the absent parent's last known address, and ask for current information. This can probably be done by phone. Check with the county clerk to find out if phone verification is acceptable to the court, or whether written certificates of search from the two agencies are required.

g. Follow up any other lead you can think of, including contacts with unions, trade associations, or licensing agencies that may have information.

2. Choose a Newspaper for Publication

The citation must be published in the newspaper of general circulation in California that is most likely to give notice of the hearing to the missing parent. Select a daily newspaper in the area where the missing parent was last known to reside. You don't have to use a legal newspaper—that is, a special newspaper that publishes legal notices.

If the missing parent never lived in California, or if his last known residence was in another state, you still publish in a California newspaper in your area.

LOS ANGELES COUNTY NOTE.
Call the county clerk's office and ask which newspaper you should use.

3. Prepare Documents for Publication

Prepare the following documents and make three photocopies of each. Ask the county clerk for standard forms; if they aren't available, you may be able to get them from a legal newspaper. If not, make your own, using the samples below. (Chapter 2, Section D contains instructions on preparing court documents.)

1. Application and Declaration—Publication of Citation

2. Order for Publication

3. Citation to Appear

LOS ANGELES COUNTY NOTE.
In Los Angeles, the Application and Order are combined in one form, which is included in the forms packet.

(1) Application and Declaration. In the Application, you give the name of the newspaper you selected and state why that newspaper is most likely to give notice to the missing parent. Your reason might be something like "Citee last lived in the area of circulation of this newspaper. Citee is most likely to read this paper." Then you must give the results of your search, giving names of those contacted, their relationship to the missing parent, and dates and results of the search. Be sure to state that the people you contacted are the most likely to know the whereabouts of the parent.

If you know the address of the absent parent but are publishing notice because you can't make service in any of the ways discussed in Section C above, explain in the Application that service could not be made except by publication.

APPLICATION AND DECLARATION—PUBLICATION OF CITATION

1 [YOUR NAME (In Capitals)]
   [Address]
2 [City, State, Zip]
   [Your Phone No.]
3 Petitioner In Pro Per

4

5

6

7

8   SUPERIOR COURT OF CALIFORNIA

9   COUNTY OF [Your County]

10 In the Matter of the Petition of   )   NO. [Case No.]
    [YOUR FULL NAME (In Capitals)],   )
11 Adopting Parent   )   APPLICATION AND
)   DECLARATION-PUBLICATION
12 _____)   OF CITATION

13   Application is hereby made for an order directing service of the

14 citation in this proceeding on [Full name of natural parent] by publica-

15 tion in [Name of newspaper], which is a newspaper of general circulation

16 in this state most likely to give the aforementioned person notice of

17 the pendency of this proceeding. In support of this application, I,

18 [Your full name], declare:

19   I am the petitioner In Pro Per. The parents of the minor, [Full

20 name of your stepchild], who is the subject of this proceeding are [Your

21 wife's full name] and [Natural father's full name].

22   The place of residence of [Natural father's full name] is unknown

23 to Petitioner and the minor's mother. The following attempts were made

24 to locate the residence:

25   [Type in your attempts to find the missing parent. Example:]

26   I made inquiry of my spouse,_____, the natural parent

27 of the minor, who does not know the whereabouts of the citee.

28 /////////

                                -1-

1   The last known address of citee was _____. The

2   address was ascertained from the custodial parent of the minor. On

3   _____ I ascertained by inquiring at the above address

4   that the citee no longer resides there. The present residents do not

5   know the whereabouts of the citee. I inquired with neighbors to the

6   right and left of the address as to the whereabouts of citee. They did

7   not know the citee's whereabouts.

8   The following attempts were made to locate citee through relatives,

9   friends, and others likely to know the citee's whereabouts. The only

10   persons likely to know the whereabouts of the citee are:

11   John Smith, brother of citee.
         Address: 12 E. St., Anywhere, California.
12   Date of Inquiry: Feb. 10, 19__.

13   Mary Smith, mother of citee.
         Address: 43 Clover Drive, Anywhere, California.
14   Date of Inquiry: Feb. 15, 19__.

15   James Duncan, friend of citee.
         Address: 123 Oak St., Anywhere, California.
16   Date of Inquiry: Feb. 20, 19__.

17   ABC Construction Co., former employer of citee.
         Address: 567 North St., Anywhere, California.
18   Date of Inquiry: Feb. 24, 19__.

19   All of the above persons either stated that they did not know the

20   whereabouts of the citee, or did not respond to my inquiries.

21   On _____ I inquired of _____

22   Union as to the whereabouts of citee. The union has no record that citee

23   is a current member of its union.

24   On _____ I searched the following records for

25   the name of citee: _____ County Register of Voters

26   Index, and _____ County Tax Assessor. The whereabouts of

27   the citee could not be ascertained from the search.

28   /////////

-2-

1   A report from the California Department of Motor Vehicles is at-

2   tached to this declaration. [If the absent parent has never resided in the State of

3   California, state: "a report by the Department of Motor Vehicles is not re-

4   quired because the citee has never resided in the State of California."]

5   WHEREFORE, Petitioner prays that the court issue its order direct-

6   ing service of the citation on [Natural parent's full name] by publica-

7   tion in [Name of newspaper] once a week for four successive weeks as

8   provided in Section 235(b) of the Civil Code.

9   I declare under penalty of perjury that the foregoing is true and

10   correct and that this declaration was executed on [Date you sign the

11   application] at [City in which you sign], California.

12

13   Dated: _____

14   [Your signature] _____
                                     Petitioner

15

16

17

18

19

20

21

22

23

24

25

26

27

28

-3-

Attach the originals you get from Motor Vehicles, Registrar of Voters, County Tax Assessor, or any other declaration from third persons regarding your search for the missing parent. Keep a copy of each for your records.

(2) Order for Publication. Next, prepare an Order for Publication. The judge will sign it when she approves your application. A sample is shown below.

(3) Citation to Appear. The third document is the citation that will be published in the newspaper. Below is a sample, with instructions. Remember that you will have to leave blank spaces for the date and time of the hearing; the county clerk will fill them in when the hearing is scheduled and the clerk approves your citation for publication (section 5 below).

4. Get Your Order for Publication Signed

Next, you must take your application, order and citation to the county clerk. Ask the clerk of the Presiding Judge[3] of the Superior Court when you can get the Order for Publication signed. The clerk may simply have you give him the documents and not require that you see the judge, or the judge may wish to talk to you personally. If you are to see the judge, bring your spouse in case the judge wants to ask both of you questions about the missing parent. Bring the originals and photocopies of:

- Application and Declaration

- Order for Publication

- Citation to Appear

 The period of time from the beginning of your search to the date the Order for Publication is submitted to the judge for signing should not be over 90 days; otherwise your search could be considered obsolete.

---

[3] The Superior Court has many judges; however, one judge is designated as the Presiding Judge, and she is probably the one who will review your Application for Publication and sign the Order for Publication. A different judge, however, may be assigned to hear your petition.

ORDER FOR PUBLICATION

1 | [YOUR NAME (In Capitals)]
  | [Address]
2 | [City, State, Zip]
  | [Your Phone No.]
3 | Petitioner In Pro Per

4

5

6

7

8   SUPERIOR COURT OF CALIFORNIA

9   COUNTY OF [Your County]

10 | In the Matter of the Petition of   ) No. [Case No.]
   | [YOUR FULL NAME (In Capitals)],   )
11 | Adopting Parent   ) ORDER FOR PUBLICATION
   | _____) OF CITATION
12

13   On reading the declaration of [Your full name] on file herein and

14 it satisfactorily appearing to me therefrom that the residence of [Full

15 name of natural father], the father of the minor who is the subject of

16 the petition filed herein, is unknown to Petitioner,

17   IT IS ORDERED that service of the citation in this matter be made

18 on [Full name of natural father] by publication in [Name of newspaper],

19 which is hereby designated as the newspaper most likely to give notice

20 to [Full name of natural father]. Publication is to be made at least

21 once each week for four successive weeks.

22   IT IS FURTHER ORDERED that a copy of the citation be forthwith

23 mailed to such citee if citee's address is ascertained before the expi-

24 ration of the time prescribed for publication of the citation.

25

26 Dated: _____

27

28   _____
                               Judge of the Superior Court

-1-

CITATION

1	[YOUR NAME (In Capitals)]
	[Address]
2	[City, State, Zip]
	[Your Phone No.]
3	Petitioner In Pro Per
4	
5	
6	
7	
8	SUPERIOR COURT OF CALIFORNIA
9	COUNTY OF [Your County]
10	In the Matter of the Petition of) No. [Case No.]
	[YOUR FULL NAME (In Capitals)],)
11	On Behalf of) CITATION TO APPEAR
	[CHILD'S FULL NAME (In Capitals)],)
12	a minor)
13	_____)
14	The People of the State of California
15	To [Full name of natural father]:
16	By order of this court you are hereby cited to appear before the
17	judge presiding in Department [Department No.*] of this court on [Month,
18	day and year of the hearing], at [time of day of the hearing], then and
19	there to show cause, if any you have, why the petition of [Your full
20	name] for the adoption of [Your stepchild's full name], your minor
21	child, should not be granted.
22	The address of the above court is [Address of the court].
23	Dated:_____
24	[Leave a space here about _____, Clerk
	1-1/2 inches square for
25	the county clerk's seal.] By:_____
26	Deputy Clerk
27	
28	

-1-

* The county clerk may not be able to give in advance the Department Number of the judge who will hear the petition. In this case ask for the Department Number of the Presiding Judge and place that number in the citation, adding in parentheses "(or as assigned)." Example: ". . . the judge presiding in Department 4 (or as assigned) of this court . . . ."

LOS ANGELES COUNTY NOTE.
After you take the Application and Order and Citation to the county clerk (central office), the clerk will get the order signed, set a date for the hearing, arrange for publication, and approve the citation. You should notify the Department of Adoptions worker of the hearing date, and then skip to Section 7 below.

5. Arrange for Your Hearing Date

After the judge signs the Order for Publication, see the county clerk and do the following:

a. File the Application and Declaration and the Order for Publication.

b. Have a hearing date set for approximately 2-1/2 months in the future, and notify Social Service of the date.

c. Ask the clerk to fill in the hearing date and Department Number on the citation and the photocopies. The clerk will approve the citation and stamp or emboss the original with a special seal. Take back the original, which will be filed with the county clerk after publication (see Section 7 below), and the photocopies.

6. Arrange for Publication

 LOS ANGELES COUNTY NOTE.
In Los Angeles County, the clerk will arrange for publication. The newspaper, however, may not start publication until you pay the publication fee; check this out with the newspaper in advance. Do not let publication be delayed because of non-payment.

The next step is to have the citation published immediately. Give the newspaper a copy (not the original) of the citation, unless the newspaper will file the original citation with the county clerk after publication. Many newspapers do the filing for you. Be sure to find out the newspaper's policy before you publish.

Publication may cost up to $100. You must pay in advance.

The citation must be published at least once each week for four successive weeks. Service of the citation by publication is not considered complete until seven days after the date of the fourth and last publication (about four weeks after the date of first publication). After service of the citation by publication is complete, there must be at least another 10 days before the hearing date (30 days in Los Angeles County). We call this period the "additional notice period." Check with the county clerk regarding the additional notice period in your county. If the additional notice period is 10 days, you must make sure the first publication date is at least 40 days before the hearing date. In Los Angeles County, the first publication date must be at least 60 days before the hearing date. It's obviously important that you not delay in ordering publication after you get your citation approved. Tell the newspaper to publish immediately, and when service must be complete.

7. Verify Publication

After the last publication, the newspaper will send you a verification of publication. If the newspaper has agreed to file the original citation for you, check with the county clerk before the hearing to make sure the citation is filed. If the newspaper has not agreed to file the original citation, fill out a Proof of Service form (photocopy the one in the Appendix) and attach the newspaper's verification statement. Then staple the Proof of Service to the original citation. File the original citation with the county clerk.

After the publication, you must also prepare and file a declaration stating that the address of the citee was not ascertained before the expiration of the publication period. Do not sign or file this declaration until seven days after the date of the fourth and last publication. A declaration is shown below.

DECLARATION OF INABILITY TO ASCERTAIN ADDRESS

ATTORNEY OR PARTY WITHOUT ATTORNEY *(Name and Address)*:	TELEPHONE NO.:	FOR COURT USE ONLY
[YOUR NAME (in capitals)] [Your phone #] [Your address] [City, State, Zip Code] ATTORNEY FOR *(Name)*: Petitioner in Pro Per		

NAME OF COURT: SUPERIOR COURT OF CALIFORNIA STREET ADDRESS: [Address of court] MAILING ADDRESS: [Mailing address of court] CITY AND ZIP CODE: [City, Zip Code] BRANCH NAME: [Branch name]	
PLAINTIFF/PETITIONER: [YOUR FULL NAME (in capitals)] DEFENDANT/RESPONDENT:	

DECLARATION	CASE NUMBER: [Case no. of the "Willful Failure" action]

DECLARATION OF INABILITY TO ASCERTAIN ADDRESS

I, [Your full name], declare that I am the petitioner in this proceeding. During the period of publication of the citation ordered by the court, the address of the citee, [Full name of missing parent], was not ascertained.

I declare under penalty of perjury under the laws of the State of California that the foregoing is true and correct.

Date: [Date you sign]

........[Your name]........................   ▶   [Your signature]
(TYPE OR PRINT NAME)   (SIGNATURE OF DECLARANT)

[X] Petitioner/Plaintiff [ ] Respondent/Defendant [ ] Attorney
[ ] Other *(specify)*:

(See reverse for a form to be used if this declaration will be attached to another court form before filing)

Form Approved by the
Judicial Council of California
MC-030 (New January 1, 1987)   **DECLARATION**

C-116

If you do discover the address of the missing parent during the publication period, mail a copy of the citation to him via registered mail. Make out a Proof of Service form and attach the registration receipt. Then prepare a declaration along the lines of the one shown just below.

E.   PREPARE A DECLARATION RE MILITARY SERVICE

Before the adoption hearing, or at it, you must file a document called a Declaration re Military Service. This declaration can be made by anyone (most likely your spouse) who can declare with reasonable certainty that the absent parent is not in military service.

Some courts may not accept a declaration by itself as adequate proof that the missing parent is not in the military service. If your court requires it, attach certificates from the services showing that the parent isn't in the military. See Section D3(a) above.

Instructions for Declaration re Military Service

Since the whereabouts of the missing parent are unknown the questions regarding the citee's address, occupation, and employer will have to be answered with "unknown."

If you obtain certificates of search, attach them to the declaration and state, in the space at the bottom of page 1, that they are attached.

If the declaration is being made without the military search certificates, it is important for your spouse to give all information leading to the conclusion that the citee is not in military service. Examples of supporting facts are:

1. Citee is disabled or physically unacceptable to the military.

2. Citee received a dishonorable or undesirable discharge from the military.

3. Citee was not in the military when your spouse last saw him and the citee would be too old to have been accepted for reenlistment.

4. Citee is a conscientious objector.

DECLARATION—CITEE'S ADDRESS ASCERTAINED

ATTORNEY OR PARTY WITHOUT ATTORNEY *(Name and Address)*:	TELEPHONE NO.:	FOR COURT USE ONLY
[YOUR NAME (in capitals)] [Your phone #] [Your address] [City, State, Zip Code]		

ATTORNEY FOR *(Name)*: Petitioner in Pro Per

NAME OF COURT:	SUPERIOR COURT OF CALIFORNIA
STREET ADDRESS:	[Address of court]
MAILING ADDRESS:	[Mailing address of court]
CITY AND ZIP CODE:	[City, Zip Code]
BRANCH NAME:	[Branch name]

PLAINTIFF/PETITIONER: [YOUR FULL NAME (in capitals)]

DEFENDANT/RESPONDENT:

DECLARATION	CASE NUMBER: [Case no. of the "Willful Failure" action]

DECLARATION—CITEE'S ADDRESS ASCERTAINED

    I, [Your full name], declare that I am the petitioner in this proceeding. The address of the Citee, [Name of Citee], having been ascertained during the period of publication of the citation ordered by the court, I mailed a copy of the citation to the Citee at [Citee's address] by registered United States mail, postage prepaid on [Date].

I declare under penalty of perjury under the laws of the State of California that the foregoing is true and correct.

Date: [Date you sign]

.......[Your name]......................   ▶   [Your signature]
         (TYPE OR PRINT NAME)   (SIGNATURE OF DECLARANT)

[X] Petitioner/Plaintiff ☐ Respondent/Defendant ☐ Attorney
☐ Other *(specify)*:

(See reverse for a form to be used if this declaration will be attached to another court form before filing)

Form Approved by the
Judicial Council of California   **DECLARATION**
MC-030 [New January 1, 1987]

C-116

DECLARATION

NAME, ADDRESS, AND TELEPHONE NUMBER
OF ATTORNEY(S)

ATTORNEY(S)

SUPERIOR COURT OF CALIFORNIA, COUNTY OF

In the Matter of the Adoption Petition of

CASE NUMBER

AFFIDAVIT/CERTIFICATE/DECLARATION
RE MILITARY SERVICE

In adoption and related matters

Adopting Parent(s)

STATE OF CALIFORNIA, COUNTY OF

I, ...,....................... .... say:
   (affiant's name)

I am (not)* a party to this proceeding
I reside at ....
My occupation is ....
I personally (know) (do not know)* the citee ....
   (name of citee · including aliases)

....

I have known said citee ....
   (approximate period of time)

The present known address of said citee is ....
....
The occupation of said citee is ....
The name of said citee's employer is ....
....
I last saw citee on .... day of .... , 19 ....
The approximate age of said citee is .... years.
The known physical incapacity of said citee is ....
....

(Strike out inappropriate words.)

Other known facts tending to show said citee is not in military service are:

(See Reverse Side)

AFFIDAVIT/CERTIFICATE/DECLARATION RE MILITARY SERVICE
In adoption and related matters

DECLARATION (page 2)

I (know) (have been unable to determine whether)* said citee (is) (is not)* in military service on active duty as a member of the Army of the United States, or of the United States Navy, or of the United States Marine Corps, or of the United States Coast Guard, or of any Department of the United States Air Force.

_____
* *(Strike out inappropriate words.)*

AFFIDAVIT**

_____

Dated: _____ , 19 ___

Subscribed and sworn to before me

Dated: _____ , 19 ___

_____
Notary Public in and for the County of
, State of California

DECLARATION**

I certify (or declare) under penalty of perjury that the foregoing is true and correct

Executed at _____ , California

Dated: _____ , 19 ___

_____
Signature of Declarant

_____
**This form is designed for use either as an affidavit or an unsworn statement made under penalty of perjury. If an affidavit, affiant should sign where indicated at the left. If an unsworn statement, he should sign where indicated at the right. DECLARATION TO BE SIGNED ONLY IF DECLARANT IS WITHIN THE STATE OF CALIFORNIA.*

NOTE 1: "Any person who shall make or use an affidavit (or declaration) required under this section knowing it to be false shall be guilty of a misdemeanor and shall be punishable by imprisonment not to exceed one year or by fine not to exceed $1,000 or both." Soldiers' and Sailors' Civil Relief Act of 1940, as amended.

NOTE 2: Certificates may be obtained from each of the Armed Services for a fee by writing the following branches; United States Air Force, Department of the Army, United States Marine Corps and United States Coast Guard. The correct addresses for inquiry may be obtained from the local offices of these branches.

If five (5) reports from the Military Service have been received, attach same to this affidavit/declaration.

F. THE ADOPTION HEARING

Sections E and F of Chapter 4 discuss scheduling the adoption hearing and preparing the adoption decree and adoption agreement, which you will need to have at the hearing. Be sure to read them so that you don't show up at the hearing without these documents, which are essential to approval of your adoption petition. Samples of the agreement and decree are shown below. (Be sure to use the samples in this chapter, which are tailored to an adoption based on "willful failure.")

 LOS ANGELES COUNTY NOTE.
You do not need to fill out an adoption agreement in Los Angeles County. At the hearing, the court will give you an agreement, called a "Consent and Agreement," to sign.

 This document is worded as though you are a stepfather. If you are a stepmother, change the words father to mother, mother to father, wife to husband, and husband to wife. Also watch out for his, him, and her.

Neither you or your stepchild should sign this form until you are at the hearing.

Some special rules apply to the hearing, because you must prove the absent spouse's "willful failure" to fulfill his parental duties. Proving "willful failure" shouldn't be too difficult, but it will take some preparation. The sworn testimony of you and your spouse carries quite a bit of weight, but you will want to go to the hearing with supporting evidence from other persons as well. Because the missing parent has not been paying child support, your spouse has probably turned the matter over to the District Attorney's office for collection. The fact that the D.A.'s office has not been able to make contact with the missing parent will help to substantiate your allegation. Ask the D.A.'s office to give you a written statement regarding its inability to locate the missing parent and how long it has been looking. Sworn declarations from close relatives of the missing parent, stating that his whereabouts have been unknown by them for over a year, will also help your case. A sample declaration is shown below. If the judge is still not convinced after you present your case, she will probably tell you where your evidence is weak and give you a chance to come back to a rehearing with stronger evidence.

ADOPTION DECREE

```
 1   [YOUR NAME (In Capitals)]
     [Address]
 2   [City, State, Zip]
     [Your Phone No.]
 3   Petitioner In Pro Per

 4

 5

 6

 7

 8                    SUPERIOR COURT OF CALIFORNIA

 9                    COUNTY OF [Your County]

10   In the Matter of the        )   No. [Case No.]
     Adoption Petition of        )
11   [YOUR FULL NAME (In Capitals)]  )   DECREE OF ADOPTION
     Adopting Parent             )   (Stepparent)
12   _____  )

13       The petition of [Your Full Name] for the adoption of [Your

14   stepchild's present full name], a minor, came on regularly for hearing;

15   Petitioner In Pro Per, his wife and the minor having appeared in person

16   before the court; and the court having examined each of them separately;

17   and evidence both oral and documentary having been introduced, the court

18   now finds that:

19       All of the allegations in the petition are true; Petitioner and

20   [Full name of your wife], the natural mother, were married on [Date of

21   your marriage to your wife], and they are now husband and wife; Peti-

22   tioner is an adult; the minor child was born on [Your stepchild's birth-

23   date] and now resides in [Your county] County, California with Peti-

24   tioner and [his or her] mother.

25       The mother of the minor was awarded the custody of the minor under

26   judgment of dissolution entered on [Date your wife's Interlocutory

27   Judgment of Dissolution was entered.*] in case No. [Case number on the

28   judgment of dissolution or annulment.] in the Superior Court of
```

-1-

* The custody order is usually part of the interlocutory or final dissolution judgment; however, if custody was awarded in a later modification of the original judgment, give the title and date of the custody order.

If custody was originally awarded to the natural father, but he executed a private written agreement giving custody to your wife, substitute this sentence in place of the third paragraph in the decree: "The mother of the minor has custody of the minor under a written agreement with the natural father."

1 California of [County where divorce occurred] (If the divorce occurred out of

2 state, substitute the name and place of the court.) County, and that the mother of the

3 minor consents to the adoption of the minor by Petitioner.

4   The natural father of the minor has willfully failed for a period

5 of more than one year to communicate with and to pay for the care,

6 support, and education of the minor when able to do so; and that cita-

7 tion has been fully served on him in the form and manner prescribed by

8 law, and his having failed to appear; and that pursuant to Section 9001

9 of the Family Code the [Your county] County Welfare Department [Substitute

10 Probation Department in place of Welfare Department, if appropriate, or Los Angeles Depart-

11 ment of Adoptions if yours is an L.A. Petition.] has made an investigation of this

12 case and has filed with the court a report and recommendation that the

13 petition be granted.

14   Petitioner has executed in the presence of the court an agreement

15 that the child shall be adopted and treated in all respects as

16 Petitioner's own lawful child.

17   The best interests and welfare of the child will be promoted by the

18 proposed adoption; the child is a proper subject for adoption, and

19 Petitioner's home is suitable for the child, and the petition should be

20 granted.

21   IT IS THEREFORE ORDERED that the minor child is now the adopted

22 child of Petitioner and that Petitioner and the child shall hereafter

23 sustain toward each other the legal relation of parent and child subject

24 to all the rights and duties of that relationship, including all legal

25 rights and duties of custody, support, and inheritance and that the

26 child shall hereafter be known as [New full name of your stepchild; if no

27 new name, end sentence after "inheritance."].

28 Dated:_____

                                    _____
                                    Judge of the Superior Court

                                            -2-

ADOPTION AGREEMENT

1   [YOUR NAME (In Capitals)]
    [Address]
2   [City, State, Zip]
    [Your Phone No.]
3   Petitioner In Pro Per

4

5

6

7

8   SUPERIOR COURT OF CALIFORNIA

9   COUNTY OF [Your County]

10 In the Matter of the   )   No. [Case No.]
    Adoption Petition of   )
11 [YOUR FULL NAME (In Capitals)],)   ADOPTION AGREEMENT
    Adopting Parent   )
12 _____)

13   ADOPTION AGREEMENT

14   I, the undersigned petitioner, having petitioned the above-entitled

15 court for the approval of the adoption of the minor child who is the

16 subject of these proceedings, do hereby agree with the State of

17 California and with the minor child that the minor child shall be

18 adopted and treated in all respects as my own lawful child should be

19 treated and that the minor child shall enjoy all the rights of a natural

20 child of my own issue, including the right of inheritance.

21   _____
                                    Petitioner
22 ////////

23 ////////

24 ////////

25 ////////

26 ////////

27 ////////

28 ////////

                                   -1-

[Type in the consent for your stepchild if he is 12 years of age or older. If you are adopting more than one stepchild 12 or over, pluralize the consent wording and add additional signature lines.]

CONSENT OF CHILD

I, the minor child who is the subject of these proceedings, do hereby consent to my adoption by Petitioner.

_____
[Name of stepchild]
Birth Certificate Name of Minor

Executed _____, 19____

In the presence of _____
                    Judge of the Superior Court

-2-

The following is an example of a Declaration by the petitioner referring to an attached letter from the District Attorney's office to help prove "willful failure."

DECLARATION

1	JOHN LEE DOE
	120 E. Street
2	Anaheim, California 56743
	(818) 555-1258
3	Petitioner in Pro Per
4	
5	
6	
7	
8	
9	SUPERIOR COURT OF CALIFORNIA
10	COUNTY OF ORANGE

```
 1   JOHN LEE DOE
     120 E. Street
 2   Anaheim, California 56743
     (818) 555-1258
 3   Petitioner in Pro Per

 4

 5

 6

 7

 8
                         SUPERIOR COURT OF CALIFORNIA
 9
                             COUNTY OF ORANGE
10
     In the Matter of the          )  Case No. 34532
11   Adoption Petition of          )
     JOHN LEE DOE, Adopting Parent  )  DECLARATION
12   _____   )

13
         I, John Lee Doe, declare:
14
         I am the petitioner in this proceeding. The District Attorney of
15
     Orange County, California has made efforts for over two years to dis-
16
     cover the whereabouts of Timothy Raymond Smith, the natural father of
17
     James Robert Smith, the minor who is the subject of this proceeding. The
18
     above District Attorney has been unable to find Timothy Raymond Smith,
19
     nor has Timothy Raymond Smith sent any child support payments to the
20
     District Attorney. Attached to this Declaration is a letter from the
21
     District Attorney's office verifying this Declaration.
22
         I declare under penalty of perjury that the foregoing is true and
23
     correct and this Declaration was executed on June 5, 19__, at Anaheim,
24
     California.
25
                                       John Lee Doe
26                                     _____
                                       John Lee Doe, Petitioner
27

28

                                 -1-
```

Reminder: The statute requires failure to support *and* failure to communicate. If the absent parent has communicated with the child, even if he hasn't supported him for more than a year, the parent has not willfully failed to meet his parental obligations under this law.

G. AFTER THE HEARING

Section H of Chapter 4 tells you what you need to do with your papers after the hearing.

H. CHECKLIST FOR A "WILLFUL FAILURE" ACTION

LOS ANGELES COUNTY NOTE.

For a Los Angeles County checklist, see Section I below.

1. _____ Gather personal documents listed in Chapter 2, Section D.

2. _____ Prepare the adoption petition. Make three photocopies. (Section A)

3. _____ File the petition by presenting the original and photocopies to the county clerk. (Section A)

4. _____ Call the Adoption Unit of the County Social Service Department to verify that it has received a copy of your petition from the county clerk. (Section A)

5. _____ Cooperate with Social Service when it contacts you for the adoption assessment. (Section B)

6. _____ If you know the absent parent's address, have him served with a citation and the adoption petition. (Section C)

   If you don't know the absent parent's address, proceed with publication of the notice. Check with the Social Service Department and the county clerk to determine if you should get the Order for Publication and set the hearing date before the Social Service report is filed, or if you must wait until the Social Service report is filed. If you must wait for the report, don't begin step 7 until the report is filed. (Section D)

7. _____ Try to find the missing parent. Contact the county clerk and determine if the court requires that you submit certificates of search from the five military services. If so, immediately send letters to the five military services, and start the formal search for the missing parent. If the certificates have not arrived 90 days after you started your search, get your Order for Publication and hearing date without them (if you wait longer, your search activities might be considered obsolete). (Section D)

8. _____ Choose a newspaper in which to publish notice of the hearing to the absent parent. (Section D)

9. _____ Immediately after completing the search, prepare the following documents and make three photocopies of each. (Section D)

   • Application and Declaration-Publication of Citation

   • Order for Publication

   • Citation to Appear

10. _____ Get the Order for Publication signed by the Presiding Judge. If you are to see the judge, have your spouse go with you to see the judge. Bring the forms you prepared in the previous step. (Section D)

11. _____ See the county clerk and do the following. (Section D)

   a. File the Application and Declaration and the Order for Publication.

   b. Have a hearing date set for approximately 2-1/2 months in the future.

   c. Ask the clerk to fill in the time and place of the hearing on the citation and photocopies and to approve the citation.

12. _____ Notify Social Service of the hearing date. (Section D)

13. _____ Immediately publish the citation to the missing parent. (Section D)

14. _____ After service by publication is complete (seven days after the date of the fourth and last publication), do the following: Section D)

   a. Make sure the original citation and Proof of Service are filed with the county clerk by the newspaper or by you;

   b. Prepare and file a Declaration-Inability to Ascertain Address. (If the address of the missing parent is learned before service is complete, send a copy of the citation and petition to the address by registered mail and prepare a Declaration-Citee's Address Ascertained.)

15. _____ Prepare an original and three photocopies of each of the following documents:

   a. Declaration re Military. Service (Attach the five Military Search certificates if required.) (Section E)

   b. Adoption Agreement. (Section F)

   c. Adoption Decree. (Section F)

   d. Supporting declarations to help you show the absent parent's willful failure to support the child. (Section F)

16. _____Attend the adoption hearing with your stepchild and your spouse and bring the forms and photocopies you prepared in the above step. Also bring the documents you gathered in Step 1 and your file of all documents you have filed with the county clerk. (Section F)

17. _____After the hearing, file the adoption decree, adoption agreement and the Declaration Re Military Service with the county clerk. Take back your rubber-stamped photocopies and have at least one copy of the adoption decree certified. (Section G)

18. _____Verify information on the Court Report of Adoption form, and request amendment of your stepchild's original birth certificate if you wish. (Section G)

FORMS LIST FOR "WILLFUL FAILURE" ADOPTION

Petition for Adoption

Citation to Appear

Application and Declaration—Publication of Citation

Order for Publication of Citation

Declaration of Inability to Find Address of Missing Parent

Declaration re Military Service

Adoption Decree

Adoption Agreement (includes minor's consent)

I.   CHECKLIST FOR LOS ANGELES COUNTY

Procedures are slightly different in Los Angeles County. Here is a checklist:

1._____Gather personal documents listed in Chapter 2, Section D.

2._____Prepare an adoption petition. Make three photocopies. (Section A)

3._____File the adoption petition by presenting the original and the three photocopies to the county clerk (central office). Three photocopies will be returned to you, rubber-stamped with the case number and filing date. (Section A)

4._____Call the Los Angeles County Department of Adoptions to verify that it has received a copy of your petition from the county clerk. (Section A)

5._____Immediately write a letter to each of the five military services requesting certificates of search. (Section D)

6._____Get a packet of pre-printed forms, to use during the rest of the adoption process, from the county clerk. The Department of Adoptions will tell you which particular packet you should get. (Section A)

7._____Conduct your search for the missing parent, including a local search made by a legal newspaper. (Section D)

8._____After completing the search, contact the county clerk's office and ask which newspaper the court uses for publication. (Section D)

9._____Prepare the following pre-printed forms from the forms packet: (Section D)

  a.   Application for Order for Publication (original and two copies). Attach the Declaration of Search if you got one from a newspaper.

  b.   Citation. Leave the time and place of the hearing blank. Make an original and three copies.

10._____Take the forms you prepared in the above step to the county clerk (central office) and leave them. (Section D) After the Order for Publication is signed, the court will:

  a.   Set a hearing date on the court calendar (approximately 65-80 days in the future).

  b.   Insert the time and place of the hearing on the citation.

  c.   Approve the citation.

  d.   Make arrangements with a local legal newspaper for publication. (You, however, must pay for publication.)

11._____Notify the Department of Adoptions worker of the hearing date, and cooperate with him regarding the adoption assessment. (Section D)

12._____After service by publication is complete (seven days after the fourth and last publication), do the following: (Section D)

  a.   Make sure the original citation and Proof of Service are filed with the county clerk by the newspaper.

  b.   Prepare and file a Declaration of Inability to Ascertain Address.

Note: If the address of the missing parent is learned before service is complete, send a copy of the citation and petition to the address by registered mail, and prepare a declaration stating that you sent it.

13. _____ Before the adoption hearing, prepare an original and three copies of each of the following documents:

a. Adoption Decree (This is not a pre-printed form.) (Section F)

b. Declaration Re Military Service (Attach the Certificates of Search from the five military services.) (Section E)

14. _____ Attend the adoption hearing with your stepchild and your spouse, and bring the forms you prepared in the previous step. At the hearing the court will furnish an adoption agreement (called a "Consent and Agreement") for you (and your stepchild if 12 or older) to sign. (Section F)

15. _____ After the hearing, file the adoption decree with the county clerk. Ask the clerk to certify at least one of your rubber-stamped copies of the decree. (Section G)

16. _____ Verify information on the Court Report of Adoption form, and request amendment of your stepchild's original birth certificate if you wish.

Chapter 6

Adoption Based on
Abandonment by the Absent Parent

You should use the procedures in this chapter if the missing parent has failed to communicate with or support your stepchild for a year or more. In these circumstances, the court may remove the requirement of the parent's consent to adoption. Your request that the court do so is formally known as an action "to declare a minor free from the custody and control of parent" or more commonly, as an "abandonment" action. (Family Code § 7822) The court's abandonment order severs the child legally from the parent and makes the child legally available to be adopted, irrespective of the wishes of the parent. The process is sometimes called "freeing the child for adoption."

An abandonment action is more complicated than the procedure described in Chapter 5 (a "willful failure" action) because the abandonment action is technically a separate action, completely apart from the adoption action. That means there are two petitions to file, two court orders to obtain, and two investigating county agencies involved—Social Service and the Probation Department. In addition, certain relatives of the stepchild must be personally served with formal notices informing them of the abandonment hearing. You may, however, be able to combine the abandonment and adoption hearings.

The fact that an abandonment action involves considerable paperwork shouldn' t discourage you from going ahead if, after reading this chapter, you believe your circumstances justify a finding of abandonment by the absent parent. We' ll take you through the paperwork step by step, and with a little patience and attention to detail, you should do just fine. As attorneys charge fairly hefty fees (often between $500 and $1000) when an abandonment petition must be filed along with an adoption petition, your efforts will save you a considerable sum.

A. HOW TO START: THE ABANDONMENT AND ADOPTION PETITIONS

The first step is to gather the personal documents listed in Chapter 2, Section D, and prepare an abandonment petition and an adoption petition. In the abandonment petition you allege that the missing parent has abandoned his child. Your adoption petition is based on the assumption that the court will agree. Samples of both petitions are shown below. General instructions for preparing legal documents are found in Chapter 2, Section D.

 LOS ANGELES COUNTY NOTE.
In Los Angeles, the abandonment petition is a pre-printed form supplied by the county. After you file the adoption petition, pick up a packet of pre-printed forms from the county clerk. The forms packet you will receive will contain several of each form, including the abandonment petition.

ADOPTION PETITION

1　[YOUR NAME (In Capitals)]
　　[Address]
2　[City, State, Zip]
　　[Your Phone No.]
3　Petitioner In Pro Per

4

5

6

7

8　　　　　　　　　SUPERIOR COURT OF CALIFORNIA

9　　　　　　　　　COUNTY OF [Your County]

10　In the Matter of the　　　　　　) No._____
　　Adoption Petition of　　　　　　)
11　[YOUR FULL NAME (in Capitals)],) PETITION FOR ADOPTION
　　Adopting Parent　　　　　　　　　) (Stepparent)
12　_____)

13　　　[Your Full Name], Petitioner, alleges:

14　　　1. The name by which the minor who is the subject of this petition

15　was registered at birth is [Full name of your stepchild as it appears on

16　birth certificate]. [If the child's name was changed after birth add this: Thereafter,

17　the child's name was changed to [changed name] pursuant to [court, order

18　number, date].

19　　　2. The minor child is a [male or female] born on [Birthdate] in

20　[City and state of birth]. If your stepchild is 12 or over add this:

22　[He/She] is prepared to consent to [his/her] adoption by the petitioner.

23　　　3. Petitioner is an adult person and desires to adopt the minor

24　child. Petitioner is the husband of [Full name of your wife], who is the

25　mother of the child and who has custody of the child. Petitioner, his

26　spouse and the minor child reside in [Your County] County, California.

27　　　4. The mother of the child, [Full name of your wife], was married

28　to Petitioner on [Date you married] at [City and state] and is prepared

　　　　　　　　　　　　　　　　　-1-

to consent to the minor's adoption by Petitioner, retaining all her

rights to custody and control.

   5. The consent of [Full name of natural father], the natural father

of the child, is not necessary for the adoption for the reason that the

Superior Court of California County of [Your County], in proceeding

No. _____, [Leave a blank space here. When you file this petition with the Abandon-

ment Petition, ask the county clerk to insert the Abandonment Case Number.] found the

child to be a person defined in Section 7822 of the Family Code, and the

child was declared to be free from the custody and control of the natu-

ral father.

   6. The minor is a proper subject for adoption. The welfare of the

minor will be served and the minor's best interests promoted by such

adoption. Petitioner is willing and able to care for and educate the

minor and to adopt the minor and treat [him or her] in all respects as

if [he or she] were Petitioner's lawful child.

   WHEREFORE, Petitioner prays that the court grant this petition and

decree that the minor has been duly and legally adopted by Petitioner;

and that Petitioner and minor shall thereafter sustain toward each other

the legal relation of parent and child, with all rights and duties of

that relation and that the child shall be known as [New name of your

stepchild]. [If your stepchild's name is not being changed, end the sentence after the word

relation.]

                              [Your signature] _____
                              Petitioner

///////

///////

///////

-2-

1	<u>VERIFICATION</u>
2	The statements in the above Petition are true of my own knowledge,
3	except as to the matters that are therein stated on my information and
4	belief, and as to those matters I believe them to be true.
5	Executed on _____, 19__, at _____, California.
6	I declare under penalty of perjury that the foregoing is true and
7	correct.
8	_____
9	Petitioner
10	
11	
12	
13	
14	
15	
16	
17	
18	
19	
20	
22	
23	
24	
25	
26	
27	
28	

LOS ANGELES COUNTY NOTE.

In Los Angeles County, the petitioner must include information in the adoption petition on his previous marriage(s). Add the following sentences to paragraph 3 of the adoption petition:

- If you (the petitioner) were never married previously, type this in: Petitioner was never married prior to the present marriage.

- If you were previously married, type this in (and repeat for more than one previous marriage): Petitioner was married prior to the present marriage in [City and State], on [Date]; the marriage was terminated on [Date of Final Judgment] by a judgment of [Give type of termination, i.e. dissolution, divorce, nullity] at [County, State] in [Name of Court] in proceeding no. [Case Number].

- If the previous marriage was terminated by death, say so.

These forms are worded as though you are a stepfather. If you are a stepmother, change the words father to mother, mother to father, wife to husband, and husband to wife. Also watch out for his, him and her.

You can file both petitions with the court at the same time (except in Los Angeles County). For filing instructions, read Section B of Chapter 4.

LOS ANGELES COUNTY NOTE.

In Los Angeles County, you must attach a copy of your stepchild's certified birth certificate to the original abandonment petition and give the clerk four copies of the petition.

ABANDONMENT PETITION

1 [YOUR NAME (In Capitals)]
   [Address]
2 [City, State, Zip]
   [Your Phone No.]
3 Petitioner In Pro Per

4

5

6

7

8   SUPERIOR COURT OF CALIFORNIA

9   COUNTY OF [Your County]

10 In the Matter of the Petition of   ) No.[Case No.]
   [YOUR FULL NAME (In Capitals)],   )
11 on Behalf of   ) PETITION TO
   [YOUR STEPCHILD'S FULL NAME (In Capitals)],) DECLARE MINOR FREE
12 a Minor, for Freedom From Parental   ) FROM PARENTAL CUSTODY
   Custody and Control   ) AND CONTROL
13 _____)

14   Petitioner alleges:

15   1. Petitioner is an adult person and desires to adopt [Full name of

16 your stepchild], a minor who is the subject of this petition. Petitioner

17 is the husband of [Full name of your wife], who is the mother of the

18 minor and who has custody of the minor. Petitioner, his spouse and the

19 minor reside in [Name of your county] County, California.

20   2. The whereabouts of [Full name of the natural father], the natu-

21 ral father of the minor, are unknown.

22   3. The minor child has been left by the natural father in the cus-

23 tody and control of [Full name of your wife], the mother of the minor.

24 The natural father of the minor has not communicated with the minor or

25 made any provisions for the support of the minor since [Give the date as

26 closely as you can determine], a period of over one year.

27 /////////

28 /////////

                              -1-

WHEREFORE, Petitioner prays judgment declaring that the minor child is free from the custody and control of [Name of natural father].

[Your signature]_____
Petitioner

VERIFICATION

The statements in the above Petition are true of my own knowledge, except as to the matters that are therein stated on my information and belief, and as to those matters I believe them to be true.

Executed on _____, 19__, at _____, California.

I declare under penalty of perjury that the foregoing is true and correct.

_____
Petitioner

After the petitions have been filed, wait about a week and then call the Adoption Unit of the County Social Service Department to make sure it has received copies of both the adoption petition and the abandonment petition from the county clerk. Also call the Probation Department, if it isn't the agency that handles stepparent adoptions in your county, to make sure it has copies of both petitions, too.

B.   PROBATION DEPARTMENT AND SOCIAL SERVICE REPORTS

Before the abandonment hearing can be held, the Probation Department must submit to the court its finding as to whether or not the missing parent has abandoned the child. The Probation Department does not make a recommendation regarding the adoption. It deals only with the question of abandonment. It will make a thorough investigation of the alleged abandonment, and will try to find the missing parent to get his statements.

You will receive a copy of its report. If the Probation Department submits a "no abandonment" opinion, your petition for the declaration of abandonment will probably be denied, forcing you to withdraw the adoption petition.

The Social Service Department makes its report to the court on the advisability of the adoption. It must approve the adoption before the court can order the adoption. See Chapter 4, Section C for a discussion of the Social Services assessment.

C. SCHEDULING THE ADOPTION AND ABANDONMENT HEARINGS

The adoption hearing isn' t held until the Social Service recommendation on the adoption is filed. If the Social Service Department submits its assessment at the same time or shortly after the Probation Department submits its report, the adoption and abandonment hearings can be combined. Otherwise, the abandonment hearing is held first. Before you ask the county clerk for a hearing date (see Chapter 4, Section C), talk to the social worker handling your request at Social Service to see how you should schedule the hearings.

D. PUBLISHING NOTICE TO THE MISSING PARENT

It stands to reason that the absent parent has a legal right to know about your attempt to adopt his child. So before you can have a hearing on the adoption or abandonment, you must give (or at least try to give) the absent parent a copy of your adoption petition and a citation telling him to appear at the upcoming hearing.

• If you know where the absent parent lives or works, you must try to have someone give him a notice personally. That process is discussed in Chapter 5, Section C.

• If you don' t know the whereabouts of the absent parent, you must publish notice in a newspaper. That process is discussed in Chapter 5, Section D.

Important Note on Preparing Forms: When you prepare the forms you need for publication, follow the examples and instructions in this chapter, not Chapter 5. They are worded to apply to abandonment actions.

Note on Declaration re Military Service: If your county requires certificates from the military services, stating that the absent parent is not in the military, you will prepare a Declaration re Military Service. Instructions are in Chapter 5, Section C. When you do, cross out the word "adoption" in the caption so it reads: In the Matter of the XXXXXXXX Petition of [Your Full Name In Capitals]. Also don' t forget to type in the case number of the abandonment action.

After you have conducted a search for the absent parent, the three documents you must prepare are:

• a Citation to Appear for the missing parent,

• an Application and Declaraton—Publication of Citation, and

• an Order for Publication.

Samples are shown below.

CITATION

1	[YOUR NAME (In Capitals)]
	[Address]
2	[City, State, Zip]
	[Your Phone No.]
3	Petitioner In Pro Per
4	
5	
6	
7	
8	SUPERIOR COURT OF CALIFORNIA
9	COUNTY OF [Your County]
10	In the Matter of the Petition of) No. [Case No.]
	[YOUR FULL NAME (In Capitals)],)
11	On Behalf of) CITATION TO APPEAR
	[CHILD'S FULL NAME (In Capitals)],)
12	a minor)
	_____)
13	
14	The People of the State of California
15	To [FULL NAME OF ABSENT PARENT]:
16	By order of this court, you are hereby cited and required to appear
17	before Department [Department Number] [The county clerk may not be able to give in
18	advance the Department Number of the hearing. In this case, ask for the Department No. of the
19	Presiding Judge of the Superior Court and use it, adding (or as assigned)] of the
20	above-entitled Court on [Month, day and year of the hearing] at [Time of
21	day], then and there to show cause, if any you have, why [Full name of
22	your stepchild], a minor, should not be declared free from your parental
23	control according to the petition on file herein to free the minor for
24	adoption.
25	The address of the court is: [Address of place of hearing].
26	For a failure without reasonable cause to appear and abide by the
27	order of the court, you will be deemed guilty of a contempt of court.
28	////////

-1-

1 The following information concerns rights and procedures which

2 relate to this proceeding for the termination of custody and control of

3 [<u>Your stepchild's full name</u>] as set forth in Sections 7860-7864 of the

4 Family Code.

5 (1) At the beginning of the proceeding the court will consider

6 whether or not the interests of [<u>Your stepchild's full name</u>] require the

7 appointment of counsel. If the court finds that the interest of [<u>Your</u>

8 <u>stepchild's full name</u>] do require such protection, the court will

9 appoint counsel to represent [<u>him/her</u>], whether or not [<u>he/she</u>] is able

10 to afford counsel. [<u>Your stepchild's full name</u>] will not be present in

11 court unless [<u>he/she</u>] so requests or the court so orders.

12 (2) If a parent of [<u>Your stepchild's full name</u>] appears without

13 counsel and is unable to afford counsel, the court must appoint counsel

14 for the parent, unless the parent knowingly and intelligently waives the

15 right to be represented by counsel. The court will not appoint the same

16 counsel to represent both [<u>Your stepchild's full name</u>] and [<u>his/her</u>]

17 parent.

18 (3) The court may appoint either the public defender or private

19 counsel. If private counsel is appointed, he or she will receive a

20 reasonable sum for compensation and expenses, the amount of which will

21 be determined by the court. That amount must be paid by the real parties

22 in interest, but not by the minor, in such proportions as the court

23 believes to be just. If, however, the court finds that any of the real

24 parties in interest cannot afford counsel, the amount will be paid by

25 the county.

26 /////////

27 /////////

28 /////////

-2-

1   (4) The court may continue the proceeding for not more than 30 days

2 as necessary to appoint counsel and to enable counsel to become ac-

3 quainted with the case.

4

5 Dated: _____   _____, Clerk

6
   [Leave a space here about   By: _____
7 1-1/2 inches square for   Deputy Clerk
   the county clerk's seal.]
8

9

10

11

12

13

14

15

16

17

18

19

20

21

22

23

24

25

26

27

28

-3-

APPLICATION AND DECLARATION—PUBLICATION OF CITATION

```
 1   [YOUR NAME (In Capitals)]
     [Address]
 2   [City, State, Zip]
     [Your Phone No.]
 3   Petitioner In Pro Per

 4

 5

 6

 7

 8                    SUPERIOR COURT OF CALIFORNIA

 9                    COUNTY OF [Your County]

10   In the Matter of the Petition of   )   No. [Number of Abandonment
     [YOUR FULL NAME (In Capitals)],    )   Action]
11   On behalf of                       )
     [CHILD'S FULL NAME (In Capitals)], )   APPLICATION AND
12   a Minor, for Freedom from          )   DECLARATION-PUBLICATION
     Parental Custody and Control       )   OF CITATION
13   _____)

14        Application is hereby made for an order directing service of the

15   citation in this proceeding on [Full name of natural father] by publica-

16   tion in [Name of newspaper], which is a newspaper of general circulation

17   in this state most likely to give the aforementioned person notice of

18   the pendency of this proceeding.

19        In support of this application, I, [Your full name], declare:

20        I am the petitioner, In Pro Per. The parents of the minor, [Full

21   name of your stepchild], who is the subject of this proceeding, are

22   [Your wife's full name] and [Natural father's full name].

23        The place of residence of [Natural father's full name] is unknown

24   to Petitioner and the minor's mother. The following attempts were made

25   to locate such residence:

26

27        [Type in your attempts to find the missing parent.]

28

                                  -1-
```

1
2
3
4
5
6
7
8
9
10
11
12
13
14
15
16
17
18
19
20
21
22
23
24
25
26
27
28

   WHEREFORE, Petitioner prays that the court issue its order directing service of the citation on [Natural father's full name] by publication in [Name of newspaper] once a week for four successive weeks as
provided in Section 7882 of the Family Code.

   I declare under penalty of perjury that the foregoing is true and
correct and that this declaration was executed on [Date you sign the
application] at [City in which you sign], California.

                              [Your signature]_____
                              Petitioner

ORDER FOR PUBLICATION

```
 1 │ [YOUR NAME (In Capitals)]
   │ [Address]
 2 │ [City, State, Zip]
   │ [Your Phone No.]
 3 │ Petitioner In Pro Per
   │
 4 │
   │
 5 │
   │
 6 │
   │
 7 │
   │
 8 │                    SUPERIOR COURT OF CALIFORNIA
   │
 9 │                    COUNTY OF [Your County]
   │
10 │ In the Matter of the Petition of    )  No. [Number of
   │ [YOUR FULL NAME (In Capitals)],     )  Abandonment Case]
11 │ on Behalf of                        )
   │ [CHILD'S FULL NAME (In Capitals)]   )  ORDER FOR PUBLICATION
12 │ a Minor, for Freedom from Parental  )  OF CITATION
   │ Custody and Control                 )
13 │ _____)
   │
14 │     On reading the declaration of [Your full name] on file herein and
   │
15 │ it satisfactorily appearing to me therefrom that the residence of [Full
   │
16 │ name of the natural father], the father of the minor who is the subject
   │
17 │ of the petition filed herein, is unknown to the petitioner,
   │
18 │     IT IS ORDERED that service of the citation in this matter be made
   │
19 │ on [Full name of natural father] by publication in [Name of newspaper],
   │
20 │ which is hereby designated as the newspaper most likely to give notice
   │
21 │ to [Full name of natural father]. Publication is to be made at least
   │
22 │ once each week for four successive weeks.
   │
23 │     IT IS FURTHER ORDERED that a copy of the citation be forthwith
   │
24 │ mailed to Citee if Citee's address is ascertained before the expiration
   │
25 │ of the time prescribed for publication of the citation.
   │
26 │
   │
27 │ Dated: _____
   │
28 │                                  _____
   │                                  Judge of the Superior Court
   │
   │                               -1-
```

LOS ANGELES COUNTY NOTE.
These forms are included in your forms packet.

These documents are worded as though you are a stepfather. If you are a stepmother, change the words father to mother, mother to father, wife to husband, and husband to wife. Also watch out for his, him, and her.

Directions for getting the Order signed by the judge and proceeding with publication are in Chapter 5, Sections D4 through D 7.

E. Notifying Relatives

In addition to serving the missing parent with a citation, you must serve notices of the abandonment hearing on certain other relatives of your stepchild.[1] The relatives are not ordered into court, but are given the opportunity to appear if they wish. It might be a good idea to contact them in advance to determine if any of them intends to contest the abandonment action. The relatives of your stepchild to be notified on the missing parent' s side of the family are the child' s:

- Grandparents
- Aunts and uncles
- Adult brothers and sisters (children of your spouse and the missing parent)
- Adult first cousins

You must serve all the above relatives whose whereabouts you know. Service must be made at least 10 days before the abandonment hearing. If none of the relatives' whereabouts are known to you and your spouse, prepare a declaration to that effect and file it with the county clerk.

---

[1] A copy of the abandonment petition should accompany each notice being served.

DECLARATION

I, [Your full name], declare that I am the petitioner, In Pro Per. The parents of the minor, [Full name of your stepchild], who is the subject of this proceeding, are my wife, [Your wife's full name], and [Natural father's full name].

Neither my wife nor I know the whereabouts of any of the grandparents, aunts, uncles, adult brothers or sisters, or adult first cousins of my stepchild, [stepchild's full name].

I declare under penalty of perjury under the laws of the State of California that the foregoing is true and correct.

Date: [Date you sign]

......[Your name]......................
(TYPE OR PRINT NAME)

▶   [Your signature]
(SIGNATURE OF DECLARANT)

[X] Petitioner/Plaintiff   [ ] Respondent/Defendant   [ ] Attorney
[ ] Other *(specify)*:

(See reverse for a form to be used if this declaration will be attached to another court form before filing)

Form Approved by the
Judicial Council of California
MC-030 (New January 1, 1987)

DECLARATION

C-116

LOS ANGELES COUNTY NOTE. In Los Angeles County, you are required to formally notify only one relative of the hearing. However, relatives not notified, where notification is possible, may have the right to appeal to the court to request that they not be bound by the adoption order and thereby maintain their legal status as the child's relatives.

1. Preparing the Notices

Prepare the relatives' notices at the time you prepare the Citation to Appear for the missing parent. Make three photocopies of each original notice. Staple a blank Proof of Service form (photocopy the one in the Appendix) to the back of each original notice.

 LOS ANGELES COUNTY NOTE.
The notice to relatives form is included in your forms packet.

2. Serving the Notices

First, present the originals and the three photocopies of each notice to the county clerk and ask him to approve the notices. All copies will be approved. The original (with the Proof of Service form stapled to it) will be stamped with a special seal. The county clerk will give you back the approved original and photocopies.[2]

---

[2]When we refer to the original citation/notice or to the Proof of Service it means the same thing—the original notice/citation (with the seal) and the Proof of Service stapled to it.

NOTICE OF HEARING

1 [YOUR NAME (In Capitals)]
   [Address]
2 [City, State, Zip]
   [Your Phone No.]
3 Petitioner In Pro Per

4

5

6

7

8   SUPERIOR COURT OF CALIFORNIA

9   COUNTY OF [Your County]

10 In the Matter of the Petition of   ) No. [Case No. of
    [YOUR FULL NAME (In Capitals)],   ) Abandonment Action]
11 On Behalf of   )
    [CHILD'S FULL NAME (In Capitals)],) NOTICE OF HEARING
12 a minor   )
)
    _____   )
13

14 The People of the State of California

15 To [Full name of relative]:

16   By order of this court you are hereby advised that you may appear

17 before the judge presiding in Department [Department No.] [The county clerk

18 may not be able to give in advance the Department Number of the hearing. In this case, ask for

19 the Department No. of the Presiding Judge of the Superior Court and use it, adding "(or as

20 assigned)"] of this court on [Month, day and year of the hearing] at

21 [Time of day], then and there to show cause, if any you have, why [Full

22 name of your stepchild], a minor, should not be declared free of the

23 custody and control of [Natural father's full name] for the purpose of

24 freeing the minor for adoption.

25   The address of the place of the above hearing is [Address of place

26 of hearing].

27   The following information concerns rights and procedures which

28 relate to this proceeding for the termination of custody and control of

                                    -1-

1 [Your stepchild's full name] as set forth in Section 237.5 of the Civil

2 Code.

3   (1) At the beginning of the proceeding the court will consider

4 whether or not the interest of [Your stepchild's full name] require the

5 appointment of counsel. If the court finds that the interests of [Your

6 stepchild's full name] do require such protection, the court will ap-

7 point counsel to represent [him/her], whether or not [he/she] is able to

8 afford counsel. [Your stepchild's full name] will not be present in

9 court unless [he/she] so requests or the court so orders.

10   (2) If a parent of [Your stepchild's full name] appears without

11 counsel and is unable to afford counsel, the court must appoint counsel

12 for the parent, unless the parent knowingly and intelligently waives the

13 right to be represented by counsel. The court will not appoint the same

14 counsel to represent both [Your stepchild's full name] and [his/her]

15 parent.

16   (3) The court may appoint either the public defender or private

17 counsel. If private counsel is appointed, he or she will receive a

18 reasonable sum for compensation and expenses, the amount to be paid by

19 the real parties in interest, but not by the minor, in such proportions

20 as the court believes to be just. If, however, the court finds that any

21 of the real parties in interest cannot afford counsel, the amount will

22 be paid by the county.

23   (4) The court may continue the proceeding for not more than 30 days

24 as necessary to appoint counsel and to enable counsel to become

25 acquainted with the case.

26 Dated: _____

27 [Leave a space here about   _____, Clerk
1-1/2 inches square for

28 the county clerk's seal]   By: _____
                      Deputy Clerk

-2-

A file-endorsed copy of the abandonment petition must be attached to each notice. Ask the county clerk for the file-endorsed copies you need.

a. Who Can Serve the Notices?

The notice must be served by someone who is at least 18 years of age and not a party to the action. This means neither you nor your spouse can do it yourself, because you are parties. The person making service can be a professional process server, or a sheriff, marshal or constable. If service can be made inside California, you can have a friend or relative do it for you. Out of state, use a professional. Whoever does serve the papers for you must fill out a Proof of Service form to prove to the court that the notices were served properly.

b. The Papers To Be Served

You must serve each relative with a copy (not the original) of the notice, together with a file-endorsed copy of the abandonment petition. The original notice is held by the server and returned to you for filing with the Proof of Service filled out.

c. Choosing the Method of Service

There are several different ways papers can be served on the relatives.

1. If relative is in California:

a. Personal service;

b. Service by mail and acknowledgment; or

c. Substituted service (service on someone else if the relative can' t be served).

2. If the relative is outside of California:

a. Personal service;

b. Service by mail and acknowledgment; or

c. Certified mail, return receipt requested.

These methods are discussed in Chapter 5, Section C.

d. The Proof of Service

This is a sworn statement that proves to the court that the required steps were actually carried out to serve the notice on the relative. The server fills out the Proof of Service, which is then attached to the original citation and filed. If you lose or misplace the original citation you will need to prepare an affidavit of "Lost Summons." A blank proof of service form is in the Appendix.

Caption: Have the server type your name and address, the name of the court, and the case number in the boxes at the top of the form. For "short title," put "Adoption Petition of [Your Name]."

Item 1:   Type in "Citation to Appear."

Item 2:   **a.** Type the name of the parent served.

b. Check the first box unless substituted service was made, in which case you should check the "other" box and type in the name of the person to whom the citation was given.

c. Type in the address of the person served.

Item 3:   Check box a (personal service), b (substituted service), or c (mailing), whichever is appropriate, and type in the date and time of service.

If box b is checked, also check the "business" or "home" box and check box (5). The server will need to attach a short statement, titled "Declaration of Diligence" and made under penalty of perjury, setting out his attempts to make personal service before he resorted to substituted service.

If box c is checked, also check either box (3) or (4). Remember to attach the return receipt or signed acknowledgment.

Box e should be checked only if the citation was published in a newspaper. If the server checks it, he should type in "publication, C.C.P. sec. 415.50. "

Item 4:   Check box a. (True, the missing parent isn' t really a "defendant," but this is a general form, not designed just for adoptions, and that' s the closest it comes to your situation.)

Item 5:   Here the server types in his name, address and phone number. If he charged a fee for serving the citation, he should enter that in 5.a. He should also check either box b or d.

Item 6:   Check this box.

Reminder: If service was made outside California, attach the professional server' s affidavit of service.

The server should sign and date the proof of service. The original should be attached to the orignal citation and filed. Make a copy for your records.

ATTORNEY OR PARTY WITHOUT ATTORNEY *(Name and Address)*:		TELEPHONE NO.:	*FOR COURT USE ONLY*
		Ref. No. or File No.	
ATTORNEY FOR *(Name)*:			

Insert name of court and name of judicial district and branch court, if any:

SHORT TITLE OF CASE:

PROOF OF SERVICE (Summons)	DATE:	TIME:	DEPT./DIV.	CASE NUMBER:

1. At the time of service I was at least 18 years of age and not a party to this action, and **I served copies** of the *(specify documents)*:

2. a. Party served *(specify name of party as shown on the documents served)*:

   b. Person served: ☐ party in item 2a   ☐ other *(specify name and title or relationship to the party named in item 2a)*:

   c. Address:

3. I served the party named in item 2
   a. ☐ **by personally delivering** the copies   (1) on *(date)*:   (2) at *(time)*:
   b. ☐ **by leaving** the copies with or in the presence of *(name and title or relationship to person indicated in item 2b)*:

      (1) ☐ **(business)** a person at least 18 years of age apparently in charge at the office or usual place of business of the person served. I informed him or her of the general nature of the papers.
      (2) ☐ **(home)** a competent member of the household (at least 18 years of age) at the dwelling house or usual place of abode of the person served. I informed him or her of the general nature of the papers.
      (3) on *(date)*:   (4) at *(time)*:
      (5) ☐ A **declaration of diligence** is attached. *(Substituted service on natural person, minor, conservatee, or candidate.)*
   c. ☐ **by mailing** the copies to the person served, addressed as shown in item 2c, by first-class mail, postage prepaid,
      (1) on *(date)*:   (2) from *(city)*:
      (3) ☐ with two copies of the Notice and Acknowledgment of Receipt and a postage-paid return envelope addressed to me.
      (4) ☐ to an address outside California with return receipt requested.   ◄ *(Attach completed form.)* ☛
   d. ☐ **by causing** copies to be mailed. A declaration of mailing is attached.
   e. ☐ **other** *(specify other manner of service and authorizing code section)*:

4. The "Notice to the Person Served" (on the summons) was completed as follows:
   a. ☐ as an individual defendant.
   b. ☐ as the person sued under the fictitious name of *(specify)*:
   c. ☐ on behalf of *(specify)*:
      under: ☐ CCP 416.10 (corporation)   ☐ CCP 416.60 (minor)   ☐ other:
             ☐ CCP 416.20 (defunct corporation)   ☐ CCP 416.70 (conservatee)
             ☐ CCP 416.40 (association or partnership)   ☐ CCP 416.90 (individual)

5. **Person serving** (name, address, and telephone No.):
   a. **Fee** for service: $
   b. ☐ Not a registered California process server.
   c. ☐ Exempt from registration under B&P § 22350(b).
   d. ☐ Registered California process server.
      (1) ☐ Employee or independent contractor.
      (2) Registration No.:
      (3) County:

6. ☐ **I declare** under penalty of perjury under the laws of the State of California that the foregoing is true and correct.
7. ☐ **I am a California sheriff, marshal, or constable** and I certify that the foregoing is true and correct.

Date:

_____
(SIGNATURE)

Form Adopted by Rule 982 Judicial Council of California 982(a)(23) [New July 1, 1987]	**PROOF OF SERVICE** (Summons)	Code Civ. Proc., § 417.10(f)

F.   THE ABANDONMENT AND ADOPTION HEARINGS

As explained above (Section C), the abandonment and adoption hearings may be combined or held separately, depending on when the Probation and Social Service departments file their reports. We discuss them separately here. If they are held together, be sure you have prepared all the documents you need before you go to the hearing.

1. The Abandonment Hearing

Before the abandonment hearing, prepare an original and three photocopies of:

- the Abandonment Order
- Declaration re Military Service

A sample order is shown below. A sample declaration is shown in Chapter 5, Section D.

Attend the abandonment hearing with your spouse and stepchild. Take the abandonment order and declaration, your copy of the abandonment petition, and any witnesses who can help show that your stepchild was abandoned by the absent parent.

Like the adoption hearing, the abandonment hearing should be brief. The judge will probably rely primarily on the probation department report.

2. The Adoption Hearing

Sections E and F of Chapter 4 tell you how the adoption hearing will be conducted. Be sure to read them before the hearing.

Before the hearing, you must prepare two documents:

1. Adoption agreement

2. Adoption decree

A sample of the decree is shown below. See Chapter 4, Section F for a sample agreement.

ABANDONMENT ORDER

1	[YOUR NAME (In Capitals)]
	[Address]
2	[City, State, Zip]
	[Your Phone No.]
3	Petitioner In Pro Per
4	
5	
6	
7	
8	SUPERIOR COURT OF CALIFORNIA
9	COUNTY OF [Your County]

```
10   In the Matter of the Petition of    )  No.[Case No.]
     [YOUR FULL NAME (In Capitals)],     )
11   on Behalf of                        )  ORDER DECLARING MINOR
     [CHILD'S FULL NAME (In Capitals)],  )  FREE FROM PARENTAL
12   a Minor                             )  CUSTODY AND CONTROL
                                         )
13   _____ )
```

14   The petition of [Your name] for the order of this court declaring

15   [Full name of your stepchild], a minor, free from the parental control

16   of [Full name of natural father], came on regularly to be heard on [Date

17   of hearing]. Having examined Petitioner, the minor child, and other

18   witnesses, and other evidence both oral and documentary having been

19   introduced, and good cause appearing therefrom, this court finds:

20   1. All of the allegations in the petition are true.

21   2. Notice of the hearing on the petition was given as prescribed by

22   law.

23   3. The Juvenile Probation Officer of [Your county] County,

24   California, has filed a written report of investigation of the

25   circumstances of the minor child, including a favorable recommendation

26   to declare the minor child free from the custody and control of [Full

27   name of natural father].

28   /////////

-1-

1 | IT IS HEREBY ORDERED that the minor child is freed from the custody

2 | and control of [Full name of natural father].

3

4 | Dated:_____

5 | _____
    | Judge of the Superior Court

6

7

8

9

10

11

12

13

14

15

16

17

18

19

20

21

22

23

24

25

26

27

28

ADOPTION DECREE

```
1   [YOUR FULL NAME (In Capitals)]
    [Address]
2   [City, State, Zip]
    [Your Phone No.]
3   Petitioner In Pro Per

4

5

6

7

8                   SUPERIOR COURT OF CALIFORNIA

9                    COUNTY OF [Your County]

10  In the Matter of the          )  No. [Case No.]
    Adoption Petition of          )
11  [YOUR FULL NAME (In Capitals)],  )  DECREE OF ADOPTION
    Adopting Parent               )  (Stepparent)
12  _____)

13      The petition of [Your full name] for the adoption of [Full name of

14  your stepchild], a minor, came on regularly for hearing; the petitioner

15  In Pro Per, his wife and the minor having appeared in person before the

16  court; and the court having examined each of them separately; and evi-

17  dence both oral and documentary having been introduced, the court now

18  finds that:

19      All of the allegations in the petition are true; the petitioner and

20  [Full name of your wife], the natural mother were married on [Date you

21  married your wife], and they are now husband and wife; the petitioner is

22  an adult; the minor child was born on [Birthdate of your stepchild] and

23  now resides in [Your county] County, California with the petitioner and

24  [his or her] mother.

25      The consents required by law under the facts of this case have been

26  fully and freely given, and filed in the manner required by law.

27      The Superior Court of California, County of [Your county] in

28  proceeding No. [Case No. on Abandonment Petition] found the child to be
```

-1-

1   a person defined in Section 7822 of the Family Code, and the child was

2   declared to be free from the custody and control of [his or her] natural

3   father.

4   Pursuant to Section 9001 of the Family Code, the [Your county]

5   County Welfare Department [Substitute Probation Department in place of Welfare

6   Department, if appropriate, or Los Angeles County Department of Adoptions if yours is an L.A.

7   petition.] has made an investigation of this case and has filed with the

8   court a report and recommendation that the petition be granted.

9   The petitioner has executed in the presence of the court the requi-

10 site consent and agreement that the minor shall be adopted and treated

11 in all respects as the petitioner's own lawful child; and the court,

12 being satisfied that the interest and welfare of the minor will be

13 promoted by the adoption proposed; and that the petition should be

14 granted,

15   IT IS THEREFORE ORDERED that the minor child is now the adopted

16 child of the petitioner and that the petitioner and the child shall

17 hereafter sustain toward each other the legal relation of parent and

18 child subject to all the rights and duties of that relationship, includ-

19 ing all legal rights and duties of custody, support, and inheritance and

20 that the child shall hereafter be known as [New name of your stepchild].

21 [If your stepchild's name is not being changed, end the sentence after the word "inheritance."]

22

23 Dated: _____

24   _____

25   Judge of the Superior Court

26

27

28

-2-

LOS ANGELES COUNTY NOTE.
You do not need to prepare an adoption agreement; the court will furnish one at the hearing.

This document is worded as though you are a stepfather. If you are a stepmother, change the words father to mother, mother to father, wife to husband and husband to wife. Also watch out for his, him and her.

G. After the Hearings

If the abandonment hearing is held before the adoption hearing, you should go ahead and file (with the county clerk) the abandonment order and Declaration re Military Service after the abandonment hearing. Later, after the adoption hearing is held, you will file the adoption decree and adoption agreement. Section H of Chapter 4 explains the procedure.

H. Checklist

(For a Los Angeles County checklist, see Section I below.)

1. _____ Gather documentation listed in Chapter 2, Section D.

2. _____ Prepare the adoption petition and the abandonment petition. Make three photocopies of each. (Section A)

3. _____ Present the originals and photocopies of both petitions to the county clerk for filing. (Section A)

4. _____ Call the Social Service Department to verify that it has received copies of both petitions from the county clerk. (Section A)

5. _____ Call the county Probation Department (Section A) to see that it has received copies of both petitions from the county clerk.

6. _____ Cooperate with the Probation Department when it makes its abandonment investigation and with Social Service when it makes its adoption assessment. (Section B)

7. _____ Contact the Social Service Department and ask if it will submit its adoption report to the court before the abandonment hearing. If it will, the adoption and abandonment hearings can be combined. Otherwise, you will have to schedule the adoption hearing after the abandonment hearing (discussed in step 11 below). (Section C)

8. _____Contact the county clerk and ask if the Superior Court requires that you submit certificates of search from the five military services. If so. immediately send a letter to each service. Start your search for the missing parent when you write for the certificates. If the certificates have not arrived 90 days after you started your search. get your Order for Publication and hearing date without them. If you wait longer than 90 days after starting your search to apply for your Order for Publication, your search activities might be considered obsolete. (Section D)

9. _____Immediately after completing the search, prepare the following documents and make three photocopies of each. Ask the county clerk or legal newspaper for standard forms. If there are none, type your own. (Section D):

    a.   Application and Declaration-Publication of Citation

    b.   Order for Publication

    c.   Citation to Appear

    d.   Notices to Relatives

10. _____Ask the county clerk how you get the Order for Publication signed. If you must see the judge, have your spouse go with you so she can give testimony, if needed, regarding the missing parent. Bring the forms you prepared in the above step. (Section D)

11. _____After the judge signs the Order for Publication, see the county clerk and do the following:

    a.   File the Application and the Order for Publication.

    b.   If the abandonment and adoption hearings will be combined:
        • Have a date set for the combined hearing. If the abandonment and adoption hearings will be held separately:

        • Have a date set for the abandonment hearing only.

        • Have the hearing date set for approximately 2 1/2 months in the future, to give you time to publish the citation in the newspaper.

    c.   Ask the clerk to fill in the hearing date on the citation (and photocopies) and the notices (and photocopies). Have the citation and notices (plus the photocopies) approved, taking back the originals and photocopies. The originals will be stamped with a special seal. (Section D)

12. _____Immediately publish the citation to the missing parent. (Section D)

13. _____Serve copies of the notices of the hearing on relatives of your stepchild on the missing parent' s side of the family. (Section E)

14. _____After the notices to relatives have been served, make sure either you or the server files the original notices and Proofs of Service with the county clerk. (Section E)

15. ____After the Service by Publication is complete (seven days after the date of the fourth and last publication) do the following (Section D):

    a. Make sure the original citation and Proof of Service are filed with the county clerk by the newspaper or by you.

    b. Prepare and file a Declaration-Inability to Ascertain Address.

Note: If the address of the missing parent is learned before service is complete, send a copy of the citation and petition to the address by registered mail.

16. ____Before the abandonment hearing prepare an original and three photocopies of each of the following documents (Section F):

- Abandonment Order
- Declaration Re Military Service (Attach the five military search certificates, if required.) If the certificates still have not arrived by the hearing date, state this fact on the Declaration Re Military Service. If the adoption and abandonment hearings are combined, also prepare an original and three photocopies of:
- Adoption Decree
- Adoption Agreement

17. ____Attend the abandonment or abandonment/adoption hearing with your stepchild and your spouse and bring the forms and photocopies you prepared in the above step. Also, bring the documentation you gathered in Step 1 and your file of all copies of documents previously filed. (Section F)

18a. ____If the abandonment and adoption hearings were combined:

After the hearing, file the Abandonment Order, Adoption Decree, Declaration re Military Service, and Adoption Agreement with the county clerk. Take back your rubber-stamped photocopies and have at least one of the copies of the Adoption Decree certified. (Section F)

18b. ____If the abandonment hearing was held separately:

    (1) After the hearing, file the Abandonment Order, and the Declaration re Military Service with the county clerk. Take back your rubber-stamped photocopies.

    (2) Notify Social Service of the outcome of the hearing.

    (3) When you are notified by Social Service that it has submitted the adoption report to the court, contact the Superior Court calendar clerk and ask for a convenient date for the adoption hearing.

    (4) Before the adoption hearing prepare an original and three photocopies of each of the following documents:

        - Adoption Decree

- Adoption Agreement (Do not sign this form until you are at he hearing.)

(5) Attend the adoption hearing with your stepchild and your spouse and bring the forms and photocopies you prepared in the above step.
Also bring the documents you gathered in Step 1 and your file of all documents you have filed with the county clerk.

(6) After the hearing, file the Adoption Decree and the Adoption Agreement with the county clerk. Take back your rubber-stamped photocopies and have at least one copy of the Adoption Decree certified. (Section F)

19. _____ The county clerk will have you verify information, and request an amended birth certificate if you wish, on the Court Report of Adoption form. (Section G)

FORMS LIST FOR ABANDONMENT ADOPTION

Petition for Adoption

Abandonment Petition

Citation to Appear (for missing parent)

Notice of Hearing (for relatives)

Application and Declaration—Publication of Citation

Order for Publication of Citation

Declaration of Inability to Find Address of Missing Parent

Declaration re Military Service

Abandonment Order

Adoption Decree

Adoption Agreement (includes minor' s consent)

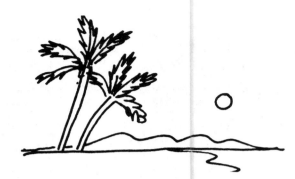

I. CHECKLIST FOR LOS ANGELES COUNTY

Procedures are slightly different in Los Angeles County. Here is a checklist.

1. _____ Gather personal documents listed in Chapter 2, Section D.

2. _____ Prepare an adoption petition. Make an original and three photocopies. (Section A)

3. _____ File the adoption petition by presenting the original and the three photocopies to the county clerk (central office). Three photocopies will be returned to you, rubber-stamped with the case number and filing date. (Section A)

4. _____ Call the Los Angeles County Department of Adoptions to verify that it has received a copy of your petition from the county clerk. (Section A)

5. _____ Immediately write a letter to each of the five military services requesting certificates of search. (Section D)

6. _____ Get a packet of pre-printed forms from the county clerk. (Section A)

7. _____ Prepare and file the abandonment petition. Present the original (with a certified copy of your stepchild' s birth certificate stapled to it) and four carbon copies to the county clerk. The county clerk will send one copy to the Probation Department, one copy to the Department of Adoptions and at least one copy back to you, rubber-stamped with the abandonment case number and the filing date. Section A)

Cooperate with the Probation Department when it makes its abandonment investigation.

8. _____ Conduct your search for the missing parent. (Section D)

9. _____ After completing your search, contact the county clerk and ask for the name of the legal newspaper the court uses for publication. Then prepare the following pre-printed forms from the forms packet. (Section D)

    a. Application for Order for Publication (original and two copies)

    b. Order for Publication (original and two copies)

    c. Citation to missing parent (leave the time and place of hearing blank and make an original and two copies)

    d. Notices to relatives (original and four copies)

10. _____ Take the forms you prepared in the above step to the county clerk (central office) and leave them. (Section D)

11. _____ After the Order for Publication is signed, the court will perform the following functions on your behalf:

   a. Have a hearing date set on the court calendar for a combined abandonment/adoption hearing; (the date should be set for approximately 65-80 days in the future.)

   b. Insert the time and place of the hearing on the citation to the missing parent and the notices to relatives.

   c. Approve the citation and the notices to relatives.
   d. Make arrangements with the local legal newspaper for publi cation. (You may have to pay the newspaper in advance, however.)

   The court will keep the original citation and will send it to the newspaper. The originals of the notices to relatives will be sent back to you approved. You will also receive an approved copy of each original.

12. _____ Serve the notices to relatives of your stepchild on the missing parent's side. (Section E)

13. _____ After the notices to relatives have been personally served, make sure either you or the server files the original notices and Proofs of Service with the county clerk. (Section E)

14. _____ After the service by publication is complete (seven days after the date of the fourth and last publication), do the following (Section D):

   a. Make sure the original citation and Proof of Service is filed with the county clerk by the newspaper.

   b. Prepare and file a Declaration-Inability to Ascertain Address.

   Note: If the address of the missing parent is learned before service is complete, send a copy of the citation and petition to the address by registered mail.

15. _____ Before the abandonment/adoption hearing, prepare an original and three copies of each of the following documents (Section F):

   a. Abandonment Order

   b. Adoption Decree (This is not a pre-printed form.)

   c. Declaration re Military Service (Attach the five military search certificates.)

16. _____ Attend the abandonment/adoption hearing with your stepchild and spouse and bring the forms and copies you prepared in the above step. Sign the adoption agreement (referred to as Consent and Agreement) provided by the court. Your stepchild, if she is 12 years or older, will also sign at the hearing. (Section F)

17. ____ After the hearing you will either be given a rubber-stamped copy of the adoption decree, or one will be mailed to you. After receiving your copy of the decree, make copies, take them to the county clerk, and ask for at least one certified copy. (Section G)

18. ____ The county clerk will have you verify information on the Court Report of Adoption form, and you may request an amended birth certificate. (Section G)

Chapter 7

ADOPTION BASED ON TERMINATING THE PARENTAL RIGHTS OF THE ABSENT FATHER

This is the procedure to use if your stepchild was born out of wedlock and if you have determined, after reading Chapter 3, Section A, that there is no legally presumed father. Under this procedure, there will be two hearings, one for the court to rule on the termination of parental rights, and then one to rule on the adoption itself.

LOS ANGELES COUNTY NOTE.
In Los Angeles, there is no separate termination of rights hearing.

A. HOW TO START: THE TERMINATION OF PARENTAL RIGHTS PETITION AND ADOPTION PETITION

You begin adoption proceedings by gathering the personal documents listed in Chapter 2, Section D and filing an adoption petition and a petition to terminate the parental rights of the alleged father. A sample adoption petition is shown below. Further instructions on document preparation are included in Chapter 2, Section D. After you prepare the petitions, make three photocopies of each.

LOS ANGELES COUNTY NOTE.

In Los Angeles, the adoption petition and termination of rights petition are filed separately. After you file the adoption petition, you will pick up forms, including one for the termination of rights petition, to use during the rest of the process.

In Los Angeles County, the petition must include information on the petitioner's previous marriage(s). Our sample petitions do not include this wording, so add this information to paragraph 3:

- If you (the petitioner) were never married previously, type this in: Petitioner was never married prior to the present marriage.

- If you were previously married, type this in (and repeat for more than one previous marriage): Petitioner was married prior to the present marriage in [City and State], on [Date]; the marriage was terminated on [Date of final Judgment] by a judgment of [Type of termination, e.g., dissolution, divorce, nullity] at [County and State] in [Name of court] in proceeding No. [Case Number].

- If the previous marriage was terminated by death, say so.

ADOPTION PETITION

```
 1    [YOUR NAME (In Capitals)]
      [Address]
 2    [City, State, Zip]
      [Your Phone No.]
 3    Petitioner In Pro Per

 4

 5

 6

 7

 8                    SUPERIOR COURT OF CALIFORNIA

 9                     COUNTY OF [Your County]

10    In the Matter of the        )  No. [Case No.]
      Adoption Petition of        )
11    [YOUR FULL NAME (In Capitals)],  )  PETITION FOR ADOPTION
      Adopting Parent             )  (Stepparent)
12    _____)

13        [Your full name], Petitioner, alleges:

14        1. The name by which the minor who is the subject of this petition

15    was registered at birth is [Full name of your stepchild as it appears on

16    birth certificate] [If your stepchild's name was changed after birth,type in this: There-

17    after, the child's name was changed to [Changed name] pursuant to:

18    [Court, order number and date of order.]

19        2. The minor child is a [male/female] born on [Birthdate] in [City

20    and state]. [If your stepchild is 12 or over, type in this: [He/She] is prepared to

21    consent to [his/her] adoption by Petitioner.]

22        3. Petitioner is an adult person and desires to adopt the minor

23    child. Petitioner is the husband of [Full name of your wife] who is the

24    mother of the child and who has custody of the child. Petitioner, his

25    spouse and the child reside in [Your county] County, California.

26        4. The mother of the child, [Full name of your wife], was married

27    to Petitioner on [Date you married your wife] at [City and state where

28    you were married] and is prepared to consent to the minor's adoption by
```

1   Petitioner, retaining all her rights of custody and control.

2   5. Under the provisions of Section 8604 of the Family Code, the

3   consent of the natural mother alone is required for the adoption because

4   there is no presumed father as determined by Section 7611 of the Family

5   Code.

6   6. The minor is a proper subject for adoption. The welfare of the

7   minor will be served and the minor's best interests promoted by the

8   adoption. Petitioner is willing and able to care for and educate the

9   minor and to adopt the minor and treat [him or her] in all respects as

10   if [he or she] were Petitioner's lawful child.

11   WHEREFORE, Petitioner prays that the court grant this petition and

12   decree that the minor has been duly and legally adopted by Petitioner;

13   and that Petitioner and minor shall thereafter sustain toward each other

14   the legal relation of parent and child, with all rights and duties of

15   that relation and that the child shall be known as [New name of your

16   stepchild]. [If your stepchild's name is not being changed, end the sentence after the word

17   "relation."]

18   [Your signature] _____
                          Petitioner

19

20   VERIFICATION

21   The statements in the above Petition are true of my own knowledge,

22   except as to the matters that are therein stated on my information and

23   belief, and as to those matters I believe them to be true.

24   Executed on _____, 19___, at _____,

25   California.

26   I declare under penalty of perjury that the foregoing is true and

27   correct.

28   [Your signature] _____
                          Petitioner

-2-

PETITION FOR TERMINATION OF PARENTAL RIGHTS

1 [YOUR NAME (In Capitals)]
   [Address]
2 [City, State, Zip]
   [Your Phone No.]
3 Petitioner In Pro Per

4

5

6

7

8   SUPERIOR COURT OF CALIFORNIA

9   COUNTY OF [Your County]

10 In the Matter of the Petition of   ) No.[Case No.]
    [YOUR FULL NAME (In Capitals)],   )
11 Adopting Parent   ) PETITION TO TERMINATE
) PARENTAL RIGHTS OF ALLEGED
12 _____) FATHER (Family Code 7622)

13   Petitioner alleges:

14   1. Petitioner, [Your full name], is an adult person and desires to

15 adopt [Full name of your stepchild], a minor. Petitioner is the husband

16 of [Full name of your wife], who is the mother of the minor and who has

17 custody of the minor. Petitioner, his wife and the minor reside in [Your

18 county] County. The mother of the minor is prepared to consent to the

19 adoption of the minor by Petitioner.

20   2. The minor does not have a presumed father under Section 7611 of

21 the Family Code, does not have a father to whom the minor is a legitimate

22 child under prior law of California, and does not have a father to whom

23 the minor is a legitimate child under the law of another jurisdiction.

24   WHEREFORE, Petitioner prays for an order of this court that the

25 parental rights of [Full name(s) of alleged father(s)] and any other

26 possible natural father be terminated and that only the consent of [Full

27 ////////

28 ////////

possible natural father be terminated and that only the consent of [Full

name of your wife], mother of the minor, be required for the adoption.

[Your signature]_____
Petitioner

VERIFICATION

The statements in the above Petition are true of my own knowledge,

except as to the matters that are therein stated on my information and

belief, and as to those matters I believe them to be true.

Executed on _____, 19___, at _____,

California.

I declare under penalty of perjury that the foregoing is true and

correct.

[Your signature]_____
Petitioner

-2-

You must next prepare a Termination of Rights Petition, in which you state that there is no legally presumed father (Chapter 3, Section A). In this petition, you ask for the court to terminate the parental rights of the alleged father and require only the consent of the mother for the adoption.

If there is more than one alleged father, the names of all of them must be included in the petition. The parental rights of those named in the petition are then terminated. Having to name possible fathers on the petition may be a distasteful thing for you and your wife to do. However, it is best to look at this requirement as a protection against anyone attempting to invalidate the adoption later. Be as thorough as possible.

Occasionally, the mother is unable to identify the father by name. The mother then must be prepared to swear under penalty of perjury at the termination of rights hearing that she does not know the identity of any possible father. The Social Service Department will probably attempt to identify the natural father for the court.

A petition for termination of parental rights is shown below.

For instructions on filing the adoption and termination petitions, see Chapter 4, Section B.

LOS ANGELES COUNTY NOTE.
After you file the adoption petition, you must pick up a packet of forms from the county clerk to use in the rest of the process. Use the forms provided instead of the sample forms in this book.

After you have filed the petitions, call the Adoption Unit of the County Social Service Department to make sure it has received copies of both petitions.

B. THE SOCIAL SERVICE ASSESSMENT

The Social Service Department of your county will make an assessment of the adoption and recommend that the court approve or deny your petitions. In a termination of rights action, if the agency doesn't approve the adoption, neither can the judge. See Chapter 4, Section C for a discussion of the evaluation process. The Social Service Department may not wish to file its adoption report to the court before the termination of rights hearing.

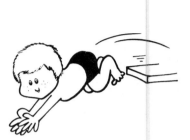

C. PUBLISHING NOTICE TO THE ALLEGED FATHER

Before the termination of rights hearing, you may have to publish a legal notice in a newspaper telling the alleged father he may appear at the hearing.

Even if an alleged father cannot be identified by name, the court may still require publication. Some judges, however, see no point in ordering a publication to an unknown father and use their discretion to waive the publication requirement. This is routinely done in Los Angeles County, but in other counties we recommend that you go ahead and publish notice. It will protect the validity of the adoption if it is later challenged by someone who claims to be the father.

1. Searching for the Alleged Parent

Before the court decides whether or not to require publication, you will have to show the court that a valid effort was made to find the alleged father. Conducting a search for the father, and documenting your results, is discussed in Chapter 5, Section D.

2. The Court's Decision on Publication

Once you have made a search and come up empty-handed, you can ask the court to allow notice by publication or to dispense with the requirement of notice to the alleged father. Sample applications for each order are shown below. If you don't know the father's identity, you may want to include a letter to the judge when you submit your application for publication. Just remind the judge that your declaration states that you don't know who the father is. The judge may then decide to dispense with publication.

If publication is ordered, you will also need to prepare:

• a citation, and

• an order for publication.

See Chapter 5, Section D for instructions on publication.

 LOS ANGELES COUNTY NOTE.
File the completed Application/Declaration and Order Dispensing With Notice (and three copies) with the county clerk.

Citation

If more than one alleged father is named in the petition, a separate citation must be published for each person named. If the alleged father cannot be identified by name, in the place on the citation where the alleged father's name would normally appear, the term "Unknown Father," "John Doe" or any other alternate the judge orders would be inserted.

APPLICATION AND DECLARATION—PUBLICATION OF CITATION

1 [YOUR NAME (In Capitals)]
   [Address]
2 [City, State, Zip]
   [Your Phone No.]
3 Petitioner In Pro Per

4

5

6

7

8   SUPERIOR COURT OF CALIFORNIA

9   COUNTY OF [Your County]

10 In the Matter of the Petition of   ) No. [Termination of
    [YOUR FULL NAME (In Capitals)],   ) Rights Case No.]
11 on Behalf of   )
    [CHILD'S FULL NAME (In Capitals)],) APPLICATION AND
12 a Minor, for Termination of   ) DECLARATION-PUBLICATION
    Parental Rights of Alleged Father   ) OF CITATION
13 _____   )

14   Application is hereby made for an order directing service of the

15 citation in this proceeding on [Full name of alleged father] by publica-

16 tion in [Name of the newspaper], which is a newspaper of general circu-

17 lation in this state most likely to give the aforementioned person

18 notice of the pendency of this proceeding, and in support of this appli-

19 cation, I, [Your full name], declare:

20   I am the petitioner, In Pro Per. The mother of the minor who is the

21 subject of this proceeding is [Your wife's full name]. The place of

22 residence of [Full name of alleged father], the alleged father of the

23 minor, is unknown to the Petitioner and the minor's mother. The

24 following attempts were made to located such residence:

25   [Type in your attempts to find the missing alleged father.]

26   WHEREFORE, Petitioner prays that the court issue its order

27 directing service of the citation on [Full name of alleged father] by

28 publication in [Name of newspaper] once a week for four successive weeks

                              -1-

1 | as provided in Section 7882 of the Family Code.

2 | I declare under penalty of perjury that the foregoing is true and

3 | correct and that this declaration was executed on [Date you sign the

4 | application] at [City in which you sign the application], California.

5 |

6 | [Your signature]
                      Petitioner

7

8

9

10

11

12

13

14

15

16

17

18

19

20

21

22

23

24

25

26

27

28

ORDER DISPENSING WITH NOTICE TO FATHER

1 [YOUR NAME (In Capitals)]
   [Address]
2 [City, State, Zip]
   [Your Phone No.]
3 Petitioner In Pro Per

4

5

6

7

8   SUPERIOR COURT OF CALIFORNIA

9   COUNTY OF [Your County]

10 In the Matter of the Petition of   ) No. [Case No.]
    [YOUR FULL NAME (In Capitals)],   )
11 on Behalf of   ) APPLICATION/DECLARATION
    [CHILD'S FULL NAME (In Capitals)],) AND ORDER DISPENSING
12 a Minor, for Termination of   ) WITH NOTICE TO ALLEGED
    Parental Rights of Alleged Father   ) NATURAL FATHER
13 _____   )

14   Application is hereby made for an order dispensing with notice to

15 the alleged natural father in this proceeding. The name of the alleged

16 natural father is [Full name of alleged father]. In support of this

17 application I declare:

18   I am the petitioner In Pro Per. The natural mother of the minor,

19 [Your stepchild's full name], who is the subject of this proceeding, is

20 [Your wife's full name].

21   The whereabouts of the above-named alleged natural father of the

22 minor are unknown to the Petitioner and the natural mother of the minor.

23 The following attempts were made to locate the alleged natural father:

24   [Type in your efforts to find the alleged father.]

25   WHEREFORE, Petitioner prays that the court issue its order dis-

26 pensing with notice to the alleged natural father.

27 /////////

28 /////////

                              -1-

1   I declare under penalty of perjury that the foregoing is true and

2 correct and that this declaration was executed on [Date you sign] at

3 [City in which you sign], California.

4

5   [Your signature]_____
                               Petitioner

6

7

8   IT IS THE ORDER OF THIS COURT that notice to the alleged natural

9 father named above or unknown natural father be dispensed with.

10

11 Dated: _____

12   _____
                               Judge of the Superior Court

13

14

15

16

17

18

19

20

21

22

23

24

25

26

27

28

                              -2-

CITATION

1 [YOUR NAME (In Capitals)]
   [Address]
2 [City, State, Zip]
   [Your Phone No.]
3 Petitioner In Pro Per

4

5

6

7

8   SUPERIOR COURT OF CALIFORNIA

9   COUNTY OF [Your County]

10 In the Matter of the Petition of   ) No. [Case No. of Termination
    [YOUR FULL NAME (In Capitals)],   ) of Rights Action]
11 On Behalf of   )
    [CHILD'S FULL NAME (In Capitals)],)
12 a minor   ) CITATION TO APPEAR
)
13 _____   )

14 THE PEOPLE OF THE STATE OF CALIFORNIA

15 To [Full name of alleged father]:

16   By Order of this Court, you are hereby advised that you may appear

17 before Department [Department number] [The county clerk may not be able to give in

18 advance the Department Number of the Judge who will hear the petition. In this case ask the

19 Department Number of the Presiding Judge and place that number in the citation adding in

20 parentheses (or as assigned)] of the above-entitled court on [Month, day,

21 and year of the hearing] at [Time of day] of that day, then and there to

22 show cause, if any you have, why your parental rights relating to [Full

23 name of your stepchild], a minor, should not be terminated according to

24 the petition on file herein to require only the consent of [Full name of

25 your wife], the mother of the minor, for adoption.

26   The address of the court is: [Address of court].

27 /////////

28 /////////

-1-

```
 1        Given under my hand and seal of the Superior Court of California,

 2   County of [Your county].

 3

 4   Dated: _____        _____, Clerk

 5   [Leave a space here about          By: _____
     1-1/2 inches square for                    Deputy Clerk
 6   the county clerk's seal.]

 7

 8

 9

10

11

12

13

14

15

16

17

18

19

20

21

22

23

24

25

26

27

28
```

ORDER FOR PUBLICATION OF CITATION

```
 1   [YOUR NAME (In Capitals)]
     [Address]
 2   [City, State, Zip]
     [Your Phone No.]
 3   Petitioner In Pro Per

 4

 5

 6

 7

 8                  SUPERIOR COURT OF CALIFORNIA

 9                  COUNTY OF [Your County]

10
     In the Matter of the Petition of   )  No. [Termination of
11   [YOUR FULL NAME (In Capitals)],     )  Rights Case Number]
     on Behalf of                       )
12   [CHILD'S FULL NAME (In Capitals)],  )  ORDER FOR PUBLICATION
     a minor, for Termination of         )  OF CITATION
13   Parental Rights of Alleged Father   )
     _____)
14

15       On reading the declaration of [Your full name] on file herein and

16   it satisfactorily appearing to me therefrom that the residence of [Full

17   name of alleged father], the father of the minor who is the subject of

18   the petition filed herein, is unknown to the petitioner,

19       IT IS ORDERED THAT service of the citation in this matter be made

20   on [Full name of alleged father] by publication in [Name of newspaper]

21   which is hereby designated as the newspaper most likely to give notice

22   to [Full name of alleged father]. Publication is to be made at least

23   once each week for four successive weeks.

24       IT IS FURTHER ORDERED that a copy of the citation be forthwith

25   mailed to such citee if citee's address is ascertained before the expi-

26   ration of the time prescribed for publication of the citation.

27   Dated:_____

28
                                    _____
                                    Judge of the Superior Court
                                         -1-
```

D. THE TERMINATION OF RIGHTS HEARING

Before the termination of rights hearing prepare the following forms and make three photocopies of each:

• Order Terminating Parental Rights of Alleged Father.

• Declaration re Military Service. (Cross out the word "adoption" in the caption so that it reads "In the Matter of the XXXXXXX Petition of [Your full name in capitals]," and type in the case number of the termination of rights action. Attach the five military search certificates if required. If the certificates still have not arrived by the hearing date, state this fact in the Declaration re Military Service.

• Declaration—Inability to Ascertain Address (see Chapter 5, Section D).

• Any declarations of third persons to support your allegation that there is no presumed father (see below).

LOS ANGELES COUNTY NOTE.
In Los Angeles, the order terminating parental rights is called "Findings and Order of the Court." The form is included in the forms packet you obtained from the county clerk. After you file the form, the court will rule on the termination of parental rights without a hearing (this is called an "ex parte" ruling).

Attend the termination of rights hearing with your spouse and any witnesses who can help prove your allegations that there is no presumed father. Bring the forms you prepared in the above step. At the hearing, the judge will sign the order that terminates the parental rights of the alleged father.

After the hearing, file the signed Order Terminating Parental Rights and the Declaration Re Military Service with the county clerk, taking back your rubber-stamped photocopies. You should also notify Social Service of the outcome of the termination of rights hearing.

ORDER TERMINATING PARENTAL RIGHTS

```
1    [YOUR NAME (In Capitals)]
     [Address]
2    [City, State, Zip]
     [Your Phone No.]
3    Petitioner In Pro Per

4

5

6

7

8                   SUPERIOR COURT OF CALIFORNIA

9                   COUNTY OF [Your County]

10   In the Matter of the Petition of )  No. [Termination of
     [YOUR FULL NAME (In Capitals)],  )  Rights Case No.]
11   Adopting Parent                  )
                                      )  ORDER TERMINATING PARENTAL
12   _____)  RIGHTS OF ALLEGED FATHER

13       The petition of [Your full name] for an order terminating the pa-

14   rental rights of [Full name of alleged father] and any other possible

15   natural father of [Full name of your stepchild], a minor, came on regu-

16   larly for hearing on [Date of hearing]. Petitioner, In Pro Per, ap-

17   peared.

18       [If you were required to publish a citation to the missing alleged father, type in this sen-

19   tence: Proof has been made to the satisfaction of the court that notice of

20   the hearing of the petition has been regularly given in the manner and

21   for the time required by law.]

22       On the testimony of [Name of your wife and anyone else who will

23   testify to substantiate your allegation] and other evidence, and the

24   court being advised in the premises, the court having found that [Full

25   name of alleged father] is not the father of the minor and is unable to

26   identify any other possible natural father, and no person has appeared

27   claiming to be the natural father of the minor,

28   /////////
```

IT IS HEREBY ORDERED that the parental rights of [Full name of alleged father], and any other possible natural father with reference to the minor, be terminated and that only the consent of [Full name of your wife], the mother of the minor, is required for adoption.

Dated: _____

_____
Judge of the Superior Court

-2-

SAMPLE SUPPORTING DECLARATION

ATTORNEY OR PARTY WITHOUT ATTORNEY (Name and Address):	TELEPHONE NO.:	FOR COURT USE ONLY
FRANK DONALD FINN (415) 555-2689 80 B Street Anywhere, California 93242		

ATTORNEY FOR (Name):   Petitioner in Pro Per

NAME OF COURT: SUPERIOR COURT OF CALIFORNIA
STREET ADDRESS: [Address of court]
MAILING ADDRESS: [Mailing address of court]
CITY AND ZIP CODE: [City, Zip Code]
BRANCH NAME: [Branch name]

PLAINTIFF/PETITIONER: FRANK DONALD FINN

DEFENDANT/RESPONDENT:

DECLARATION	CASE NUMBER: Case no. 56732

I, Mary Brown, declare that I am the mother of Jane Susan Finn. Jane Susan Finn is the wife of Frank Donald Finn, the petioner in this proceeding. Jane Susan Finn is the mother of James Peter Brown, the minor who is the subject of this proceeding.

My daughter, Jane Susan Finn, was living with me when she gave birth to James Peter Brown. The alleged father of the minor, Peter Samuels, and my daughter were never married, nor did they ever attempt to marry either before or after the birth of the minor. Peter Samuels made no communication with my daughter during her pregnancy. Nor did he make any attempt to communicate with my daughter or the minor after the birth of the minor.

I declare under penalty of perjury under the laws of the State of California that the foregoing is true and correct.

Date:

....
(TYPE OR PRINT NAME)

▶ *Mary Brown*
(SIGNATURE OF DECLARANT)

☐ Petitioner/Plaintiff   ☐ Respondent/Defendant   ☐ Attorney
☒ Other (specify):

(See reverse for a form to be used if this declaration will be attached to another court form before filing)

Form Approved by the
Judicial Council of California   **DECLARATION**
MC-030 [New January 1, 1987]

C-116

E. THE ADOPTION HEARING

After approving your petition to terminate the alleged father's parental rights, the court can act on the adoption petition without his consent. It will rule on the petition at an adoption hearing. See Chapter 4, Sections E through G, for instructions on how to schedule the hearing and prepare the adoption decree and adoption agreement, which you will need to take to the hearing. Follow the samples of these forms shown below when you type your own.

LOS ANGELES COUNTY NOTE.
To set a hearing date, you will need to file a Memorandum For Setting For Hearing. The form is included in your forms packet. You do not need to prepare an adoption agreement; the court will provide one at the hearing.

Neither you or your stepchild should sign the agreement until you are at the hearing.

F.   AFTER THE ADOPTION HEARING

Section G of Chapter 4 tells you what you need to do with your documents after the adoption hearing is over and the adoption is approved by the judge.

ADOPTION DECREE

1	[YOUR NAME (In Capitals)] [Address]
2	[City, State, Zip] [Your Phone No.]
3	Petitioner In Pro Per
4	
5	
6	
7	
8	SUPERIOR COURT OF CALIFORNIA
9	COUNTY OF [Your County]
10	In the Matter of the) No. [Case No.] Adoption Petition of)
11	[YOUR FULL NAME (In Capitals)],) DECREE OF ADOPTION Adopting Parent) (Stepparent)
12	_____)
13	The petition of [Your full name] for the adoption of [Full name of
14	your stepchild], a minor, came on regularly for hearing; the petitioner
15	In Pro Per, his wife and the minor having appeared in person before the
16	court; and the court having examined each of them separately; and evi-
17	dence both oral and documentary having been introduced, the court now
18	finds that:
19	All of the allegations in the petition are true; the petitioner and
20	[Full name of your wife], the natural mother were married on [Date], and
21	are now husband and wife; the petitioner is an adult; the minor child
22	was born on [Birthdate of your stepchild] and now resides in [Your
23	county] County, California with the petitioner and [his or her] mother.
24	The consents required by law under the facts of this case have been
25	fully and freely given, and filed in the manner required by law.
26	The Superior Court of California, County of [Your county] in pro-
27	ceeding No. [Case number of termination/rights petition] found that the
28	minor does not have a presumed father under Section 7611 of the Family

-1-

1 Code and ordered that only the consent of [<u>Full name of your wife</u>],

2 mother of the above-named minor, is required for the adoption.

3   Pursuant to Section 9001 of the Family Code, the [<u>Your county</u>]

4 County Welfare Department [Substitute Probation Department in place of Welfare Depart-

5 ment, if appropriate, or Los Angeles County Department of Adoption if yours is an L.A. Petition.]

6 has made an investigation of this case and has filed with the court a

7 report and recommendation that the petition be granted.

8   The petitioner has executed in the presence of the court the requi-

9 site consent and agreement that the minor shall be adopted and treated

10 in all respects as the petitioner's own lawful child; and the court,

11 being satisfied that the interests and welfare of the minor herein will

12 be promoted by the adoption proposed; and that the petition should be

13 granted,

14   IT IS THEREFORE ORDERED that the minor child is now the adopted

15 child of the petitioner and that the petitioner and the child shall

16 hereafter sustain toward each other the legal relation of parent and

17 child subject to all the rights and duties of that relationship, includ-

18 ing all legal rights and duties of custody, support, and inheritance,

19 and that the child shall hereafter be known as [<u>New name of your step-</u>

20 <u>child</u>]. [If your stepchild's name is not being changed, end the sentence after the word "inheri-

21 tance."]

22

23 Dated: _____

24   Judge of the Superior Court

25

26

27

28

-2-

ADOPTION AGREEMENT

1	[YOUR NAME (In Capitals)]
	[Address]
2	[City, State, Zip]
	[Your Phone No.]
3	Petitioner In Pro Per
4	
5	
6	
7	
8	SUPERIOR COURT OF CALIFORNIA
9	COUNTY OF [Your County]
10	In the Matter of the) No. [Case No.]
	Adoption Petition of)
11	[YOUR FULL NAME (In Capitals)],) ADOPTION AGREEMENT
	Adopting Parent)
12	_____)
13	ADOPTION AGREEMENT
14	I, the undersigned petitioner, having petitioned the above entitled
15	court for the approval of the adoption of the minor child who is the
16	subject of these proceedings, do hereby agree with the State of Califor-
17	nia and with the minor child that the minor child shall be adopted and
18	treated in all respects as my own lawful child should be treated and
19	that said minor child shall enjoy all the rights of a natural child of
20	my own issue, including the right of inheritance.
21	
22	[Your signature] _____
	Petitioner
23	
24	////////
25	////////
26	////////
27	////////
28	////////

-1-

[Type in the "consent of child" only if your stepchild is 12 years of age or older. If you are adopting more than one stepchild 12 or over, pluralize the consent wording and add additional signature lines.]

CONSENT OF CHILD

    I, the minor child who is the subject of these proceedings, do hereby consent to my adoption by the petitioner.

_____
[Name of stepchild]
Birth Certificate Name of Minor

Executed _____, 19___

In the presence of _____
                    Judge of the Superior Court

-2-

G. Checklist

Note: If you are filing in Los Angeles County, use the checklist in Section H below.

1. _____Gather personal documents listed in Chapter 2, Section D.

2. _____Prepare the adoption petition and the Petition to Terminate Parental Rights of Alleged Father. Make three photocopies of each petition. (Section A)

3. _____File both petitions by presenting the originals and photocopies to the county clerk. (Section A)

4. _____Call the County Social Service Department to verify that it has received copies of both petitions from the county clerk. (Section A)

5. _____Conduct a search for the alleged father. Remember to write for certificates of search from the military services if your county requires it. (Section C) If the certificates have not arrived 90 days after you started your search, get your Order for Publication and hearing date without them; otherwise your search activities might be considered obsolete.

6. _____Contact the county clerk's office to determine if your Superior Court requires publication of a citation to the missing alleged father. (Section C)

   a. If publication is not required, prepare a Declaration and Order Dispensing with Notice to Alleged Natural Father. (Remember, however, that we recommend publishing notice even if the court doesn't require it.)

   b. If publication is required, or if you can not ascertain what the court's policy is on publication, prepare these documents and make three photocopies of each:

   • Application and Declaration-Publication of Citation

   • Order for Publication

   • Citation to Appear

7. _____Ask the county clerk when you can see the Presiding Judge (or other court official) to get the Order Dispensing with Notice (or Order for Publication) signed. Have your spouse go with you to see the judge so she can give testimony, if needed, regarding your inability to find the alleged father. Bring the forms you prepared in Step 6. (Section C)

8. _____If the judge dispenses with notice, do the following: (Section D)

   a. File the Declaration and Order Dispensing with Notice with the county clerk.

   b. Ask the county clerk to set a hearing date for the termination of rights hearing.

If the judge requires publication, see the county clerk and do the following: (Section C)

a. File the Application and Declaration-Order for Publication and the signed Order for Publication.

b. Have the date set for the termination of rights hearing. Set the date approximately 2-1/2 months in the future to allow time for publication.

c. Immediately publish the citation to the alleged father.

Note: If the address of the alleged parent is learned before service is complete, send a copy of the citation and petition to the address by registered mail.

d. After service by publication is complete (seven days after the date of the fourth and last publication), make sure the original citation and Proof-of-Service is filed with the county clerk by the newspaper or by you.

9. _____ Prepare and file a Declaration-Inability to Ascertain Address and any declarations from third persons to help you show the court there is no "presumed" father. (Section D)

10. _____ Attend the termination of rights hearing with your spouse and any witnesses you want to testify. Take the documents you prepared in Steps 9 and 10. (Section D)

11. _____ File the signed Order Terminating Parental Rights and Declaration re Military Service with the county clerk. Notify Social Service of the outcome of the hearing. (Section D)

12. _____ When Social Service submits the adoption to the court, contact the Superior Court calendar clerk and ask for a convenient date for the adoption hearing. (Section E)

13. _____ Before the adoption hearing, prepare an original and three photocopies of each of the following documents: (Section E)

a. Adoption Decree

b. Adoption Agreement (Do not sign this form until you are at the hearing.)

14. _____ Attend the adoption hearing with your stepchild and your spouse. Bring the forms and photocopies you prepared in the above step, as well as the documents you gathered in Step 1 and your file of all documents you filed with the county clerk. (Section E)

15. _____ After the hearing, file the adoption decree and the adoption agreement with the county clerk. Take back your rubber-stamped photocopies and have at least one copy of the adoption decree certified. (Section F)

16. _____ The county clerk will have you verify information and request an amended birth certificate, if you wish, on the Court Report of Adoption form. (Section F)

FORMS LIST FOR ADOPTION BASED ON TERMINATION OF PARENTAL RIGHTS

Petition for Adoption
Petition to Terminate Parental Rights
Order Terminating Parental Rights
Citation to Appear
Application and Declaration—Publication of Citation*
Order for Publication of Citation*
Declaration of Inability to Find Address of Missing Parent*
Declaration re Military Service*
Adoption Decree
Adoption Agreement (includes minor's consent)

*Required only if the court orders publication of notice to the alleged father.

H. CHECKLIST FOR LOS ANGELES COUNTY

Procedures are slightly different in Los Angeles County. Here is a checklist.

1. _____ Gather personal documents listed in Chapter 2, Section D.

2. _____ Prepare an adoption petition. Make an original and three photocopies. (Section A)

3. _____ File the adoption petition by presenting the original and the three photocopies to the county clerk (central office). Three photocopies will be returned to you, rubber-stamped with the case number and filing date. (Section A)

4. _____ Call the Los Angeles County Department of Adoption to verify that it has received a copy of the adoption petition from the county clerk. (Section A)

5. _____ Get a packet of pre-printed forms from the county clerk. Be sure to make carbon copies as opposed to photocopies for these pre-printed forms. (Section A)

6. _____ Conduct your formal search for the alleged father. (Section C)

7. _____ Prepare the following pre-printed forms from your forms packet (original and two copies of each): (Section C)

    a. Petition to Determine Parental Rights of Alleged Father.

    b. Declaration and Order Dispensing with Notice to the Alleged Natural Father

    c. Findings and Order of the Court (This is the order which removes the need for consent of the alleged father.)

8. _____ File the forms you prepared in the above step with the county clerk. There is no hearing on the termination of rights issue; if the judge approves your termination of rights petition, she will sign the Findings and Order of the Court, and the original will be filed. A copy of the order will be sent to you and to the Department of Adoptions. (Section C)

9. _____ After the Department of Adoptions completes its assessment, prepare and file a Memorandum for Setting for Hearing, indicating the date you prefer for the adoption hearing. The hearing date you want will be confirmed or you will be asked to select another date. The county clerk provides the Memorandum. (Section D)

10. _____ Before the adoption hearing, prepare an original and three photocopies of the Adoption Decree. (Section E)

11. _____ Attend the adoption hearing with your stepchild and your spouse, and bring the adoption decree you prepared in the previous step. At the hearing, the court will furnish an adoption agreement (referred   to as Consent and Agreement) for you (and your stepchild, if 12 or older) to sign. (Section E)

12. _____ After the hearing, you will either be given your rubber-stamped copies of the adoption decree or they will be mailed to you. Ask the county clerk to certify at least one of your rubber-stamped copies. (Section F)

13. _____ If you have requested an amended birth certificate, a certified copy will be sent to you by the California Registrar. If your stepchild was   born in another state, the California Registrar will send you a notice advising you to contact the other state to request amendment. (Section F)

Chapter 8

LAWYERS

Most people can handle the adoption of a stepchild, start to finish, without a lawyer. But if you get stuck somewhere along the way, a lawyer may be able to help you get the job done.

A. HOW A LAWYER CAN HELP YOU

You don't have to hire a lawyer and turn the adoption over to him or her. Many lawyers will be willing to give you help along the way. If things do start getting complicated—for example, the absent parent unexpectedly decides to contest the adoption—you can always turn the case over to the lawyer.

Here are a few ways a lawyer may help during the process:

1. Negotiating With the Absent Parent

A lawyer who is a good negotiator may be able to get the absent parent to consent when you cannot. This is especially true if you and the absent parent don't get along.

2. Assisting With Preparing Documents

If you need to prepare court documents that are more complicated than the samples shown in this book, a lawyer can help you write them or go over the ones you have prepared.

3. Filing and Serving Legal Documents

A lawyer, or assistants in her office such as paralegals or legal secretaries, may be able to help you put court documents together in the right format, following any special rules or customs your local court may have. And having the lawyer's office take care of filing and serving papers may simplify the process for you.

4. Answering Questions Along the Way

You may come to particular points of confusion, where some expert legal advice can save you much time and frustration.

B. HOW TO FIND AND SELECT A QUALIFIED LAWYER

Finding a good lawyer isn't impossible, but it is likely to require some searching. Try to get several recommendations, and then talk to each one before hiring someone.

Free Legal Help: If you are poor enough, you may qualify for free legal help from Legal Aid, which is a government agency. But because legal aid offices have had their funds cut back severely, many no longer handle routine matters such as stepparent adoptions. They may, however, be able to give you limited advice, even if a lawyer won't represent you.

It probably won't be difficult to get a short list of lawyers recommended to you. Here's how to start.

Friends and Family. Ask friends or relatives who have hired a lawyer for recommendations. But be aware that because many lawyers specialize, an attorney who did a great job on your friend's bankruptcy may not know a thing about stepparent adoptions. But call anyway, and ask for a referral to a lawyer who handles family law matters.

Small Businesses. Business people almost always know and work with lawyers. And a small business person savvy enough to run a good business is likely to work with a trustworthy lawyer.

Independent Paralegals. Independent paralegals are non-lawyers who help people complete and file court papers. They do not give legal advice. They do, however, frequently refer customers to lawyers. Look in the Yellow Pages under "Paralegals" or "Typing Services," or call the National Association for Independent Paralegals at 800-542-0034 for lawyer referrals.

Bar Association Referral Services. A local bar association (lawyers' organization) may refer you to a lawyer who will give you a short consultation for a reduced fee or free of charge. Unfortunately, most bar associations don't screen lawyers; in many areas, you may get referred to someone who just needs clients.

C. LAWYERS' FEES

A lawyer may charge you by the hour, or offer to handle the whole adoption for a fixed fee. If you want a lawyer to give you limited advice, and not handle the whole adoption, the lawyer will probably bill by the hour.

Whatever your fee agreement, put it in writing. In California, if you and the lawyer reasonably expect fees to be $1,000 or more, the law requires the fee agreement to be in writing.

1. Hourly Fee

Hourly rates for lawyers who do general family law typically run from $100 to $250 per hour. Certain experts and big firm lawyers charge even more.

In addition to the hourly rate, find out exactly how the lawyer calculates the bill. For example, some lawyers who charge by the hour bill in minimum chunks of every 15 minutes (quarter hour), and others bill for every six minutes (tenth of an hour).

A lawyer may ask you to pay a "retainer"—a deposit or advance fee, which is kept in a trust account and used as services are provided. You shouldn't be expected to come up with a large amount of money, since you do not plan on running up high legal bills. Paying more than about $500 is likely excessive.

2. Fixed Fee

A fixed fee is a set fee for a particular project. Rates vary widely, but it's not uncommon for a lawyer to charge $1,200 to handle a stepparent adoption.

3. Costs

Whatever the fee arrangement, always verify if there will be any incidental fees, such as photocopy and fax charges. If there are, you may be able to find ways to cut them down. For example, if you learn the law office charges $3 or more for each page it faxes, have documents mailed to you instead. Make copies of documents yourself; lawyers often charge more than the local copy shop since they charge for the time it takes to make copies.

D. Getting the Most for Your Money

If your lawyer is charging you by the hour, here are some ideas on how to keep the bills down.

1. Prepare Before You Talk to Your Lawyer

Prepare for all sessions, including phone calls, by sending or bringing the attorney copies of all key documents.

Also put your questions in writing and mail, fax or deliver them to your attorney before meetings whenever possible. That way the lawyer can find answers if he doesn't know them off the top of his head without having to call you back and charge for a separate phone conference.

2. Consolidate Your Questions

Because hourly charges are divided up into parts of an hour, you may be charged for more time than you actually spend. For example, if your lawyer bills in 15-minute intervals and you only talk for five minutes, you may still be charged for the whole 15. So it pays to gather your questions and ask them all at once, rather than calling every time you have a question.

3. Try to Answer Questions on Your Own

Do as much as you can by yourself and turn to the lawyer only when you are really stuck. By reading this book and talking to social service workers or the court clerk, you can probably answer many questions on your own.

4. Carefully Review Lawyer Bills

Read your bill, which under law must be itemized, carefully. Lawyers make mistakes, and your charges may be wrong.

APPENDIX

COURT REPORT OF ADOPTION

STATE BIRTH CERTIFICATE NUMBER

LOCAL REGISTRATION DISTRICT AND CERTIFICATE NUMBER

PART I The information in this section must be given as it was before adoption. Without this data it may be impossible to prepare an amended certificate of birth for this child.

COMPLETE THIS FORM IN BLACK INK.

FACTS OF BIRTH

1A. NAME OF CHILD—FIRST NAME	1B. MIDDLE NAME	1C. LAST NAME

2. SEX	3. DATE OF BIRTH	4. NAME OF PHYSICIAN OR OTHER PERSON WHO ATTENDED THIS BIRTH

5A. PLACE OF BIRTH—NAME OF HOSPITAL	5B. CITY OR TOWN	5C. STATE OR FOREIGN COUNTRY

NATURAL PARENTS' DATA

6A. NAME OF FATHER—FIRST NAME	6B. MIDDLE NAME	6C. LAST NAME

7A. BIRTH NAME OF MOTHER—FIRST NAME	7B. MIDDLE NAME	7C. LAST NAME (BIRTH SURNAME)

PART II Adopting parents must furnish the following information concerning themselves as it was at the date of birth of the above child. This information is used in preparation of the amended certificate of birth.

CHECK APPROPRIATE BOX — ADOPTIVE OR NATURAL FATHER

8A. NAME OF FATHER—FIRST NAME	8B. MIDDLE NAME	8C. LAST NAME (BIRTH SURNAME)

9. BIRTHPLACE (STATE OR FOREIGN COUNTRY)	10. DATE OF BIRTH OF FATHER (ENTER MONTH, DAY, YEAR)

CHECK APPROPRIATE BOX — ADOPTIVE OR NATURAL MOTHER

11A. BIRTH NAME OF MOTHER—FIRST NAME	11A. MIDDLE NAME	11C. LAST NAME (BIRTH SURNAME)

12. BIRTHPLACE (STATE OR FOREIGN COUNTRY)	13. DATE OF BIRTH OF MOTHER (ENTER MONTH, DAY, YEAR)

INSTRUCTIONS TO STATE REGISTRAR

14. DO YOU WANT AN AMENDED BIRTH RECORD PREPARED?	(SPECIFY YES OR NO)	15. DO YOU WANT THE NAME OF THE HOSPITAL OR OTHER FACILITY WHERE BIRTH OCCURRED OMITTED, AS PROVIDED IN SECTION 10433 OF THE HEALTH AND SAFETY CODE?	(SPECIFY YES OR NO)	16. WHEN A CHILD IS ADOPTED BY AN UNMARRIED MAN OR WOMAN, SPECIFY IF THE PARENT REQUESTS THAT THE AMENDED CERTIFICATE REFLECT THE FACT THAT THE ADOPTION WAS A SINGLE PARENT ADOPTION, AS PROVIDED FOR IN SECTION 10433.1 OF THE HEALTH AND SAFETY CODE	(SPECIFY YES OR NO)

VERIFICATION OF PART II

17. SIGNATURE AND MAILING ADDRESS OF PARENT VERIFYING DATA IN PART II ▶

AGENCY OR DEPARTMENT

18. NAME AND MAILING ADDRESS OF AGENCY OR DEPARTMENT WHICH INVESTIGATED OR HANDLED CASE

ATTORNEY

19. NAME AND MAILING ADDRESS OF ATTORNEY

PART III The county clerk should require that as much of the information as is available in Parts I and II, above, be furnished before he completes Part III and forwards the report to the State Registrar of Vital Statistics.

COUNTY CLERK

20. I HEREBY CERTIFY THAT THE CHILD DESCRIBED ABOVE WAS ADOPTED BY THE ABOVE NAMED ADOPTIVE PARENT(S) ON THE _____ DAY OF _____ 19 _____ AS SET FORTH IN THE DECREE OF ADOPTION MADE ON THAT DATE. IN CASE NUMBER _____	21. DATE OF FILING OF PETITION
	22. THE NAME OF THE CHILD AS SET FORTH IN THE DECREE OF ADOPTION

23. SIGNATURE AND SEAL OF COUNTY CLERK ▶	BY:	24. DATE SIGNED	25. CLERK IN AND FOR THE COUNTY OF

NAME AND MAILING ADDRESS OF PERSON TO WHOM CERTIFIED COPY IS TO BE SENT

NAME	
STREET ADDRESS	
ADDRESS—CITY OR TOWN, STATE, ZIP CODE	

STATE OF CALIFORNIA, DEPARTMENT OF HEALTH SERVICES, OFFICE OF THE STATE REGISTRAR OF VITAL STATISTICS

VS-44 (9-82)

NAME AND ADDRESS OF SENDER	TELEPHONE NO.	FOR COURT USE ONLY

Insert name of court judicial district or branch court if any and Post Office and Street Address

PLAINTIFF

DEFENDANT

NOTICE AND ACKNOWLEDGMENT OF RECEIPT	Case Number

TO: ....

(insert name of individual being served)

This summons and other document(s) indicated below are being served pursuant to Section 415.30 of the California Code of Civil Procedure. Your failure to complete this form and return it to me within 20 days may subject you (or the party on whose behalf you are being served) to liability for the payment of any expenses incurred in serving a summons on you in any other manner permitted by law.

If you are being served on behalf of a corporation, unincorporated association (including a partnership), or other entity, this form must be signed by you in the name of such entity or by a person authorized to receive service of process on behalf of such entity. In all other cases, this form must be signed by you personally or by a person authorized by you to acknowledge receipt of summons. Section 415.30 provides that this summons and other document(s) are deemed served on the date you sign the Acknowledgment of Receipt below, if you return this form to me.

Dated: _____

_____
(Signature of sender)

ACKNOWLEDGMENT OF RECEIPT

This acknowledges receipt of (To be completed by sender before mailing)

1. ☐ A copy of the summons and of the complaint.
2. ☐ A copy of the summons and of the Petition (Marriage) and :
   ☐ Blank Confidential Counseling Statement (Marriage)
   ☐ Order to Show Cause (Marriage)
   ☐ Blank Responsive Declaration
   ☐ Blank Financial Declaration
   ☐ Other (Specify)

(To be completed by recipient)

Date of receipt: ....

_____
(Signature of person acknowledging receipt, with title if acknowledgment is made on behalf of another person)

Date this form is signed : ....

_____
(Type or print your name and name of entity, if any, on whose behalf this form is signed)

Form Approved by the
Judicial Council of California
Revised Effective January 1, 1975

NOTICE AND ACKNOWLEDGMENT OF RECEIPT

CCP 415.30, 417.10
Cal. Rules of Court,
Rule 1216

76N629R—8-77—PS 10-77
RC031

ATTORNEY OR PARTY WITHOUT ATTORNEY *(Name and Address)*:		TELEPHONE NO.:	FOR COURT USE ONLY
		Ref. No. or File No.	
ATTORNEY FOR *(Name)*:			
Insert name of court and name of judicial district and branch court, if any:			
SHORT TITLE OF CASE:			

PROOF OF SERVICE (Summons)	DATE:	TIME:	DEPT./DIV.:	CASE NUMBER:

1. At the time of service I was at least 18 years of age and not a party to this action, and **I served copies** of the *(specify documents)*:

2. a. Party served *(specify name of party as shown on the documents served)*:

   b. Person served: ☐ party in item 2a   ☐ other *(specify name and title or relationship to the party named in item 2a)*:

   c. Address:

3. I served the party named in item 2
   a. ☐ **by personally delivering** the copies   (1) on *(date)*:   (2) at *(time)*:
   b. ☐ **by leaving** the copies with or in the presence of *(name and title or relationship to person indicated in item 2b)*:

   　　(1) ☐ **(business)** a person at least 18 years of age apparently in charge at the office or usual place of business of the person served. I informed him or her of the general nature of the papers.
   　　(2) ☐ **(home)** a competent member of the household (at least 18 years of age) at the dwelling house or usual place of abode of the person served. I informed him or her of the general nature of the papers.
   　　(3) on *(date)*:   (4) at *(time)*:
   　　(5) ☐ A **declaration of diligence** is attached. *(Substituted service on natural person, minor, conservatee, or candidate.)*
   c. ☐ **by mailing** the copies to the person served, addressed as shown in item 2c, by first-class mail, postage prepaid,
   　　(1) on *(date)*:   (2) from *(city)*:
   　　(3) ☐ with two copies of the Notice and Acknowledgment of Receipt and a postage-paid return envelope addressed to me.
   　　(4) ☐ to an address outside California with return receipt requested.   ◄ *(Attach completed form.)* ➤
   d. ☐ **by causing** copies to be mailed. A declaration of mailing is attached.
   e. ☐ **other** *(specify other manner of service and authorizing code section)*:

4. The "Notice to the Person Served" (on the summons) was completed as follows:
   a. ☐ as an individual defendant.
   b. ☐ as the person sued under the fictitious name of *(specify)*:
   c. ☐ on behalf of *(specify)*:
   　　under: ☐ CCP 416.10 (corporation)   ☐ CCP 416.60 (minor)   ☐ other:
   　　　　　 ☐ CCP 416.20 (defunct corporation)   ☐ CCP 416.70 (conservatee)
   　　　　　 ☐ CCP 416.40 (association or partnership)   ☐ CCP 416.90 (individual)

5. **Person serving** *(name, address, and telephone No.)*:
   　a. **Fee** for service: $
   　b. ☐ Not a registered California process server.
   　c. ☐ Exempt from registration under B&P § 22350(b).
   　d. ☐ Registered California process server.
   　　　(1) ☐ Employee or independent contractor.
   　　　(2) Registration No.:
   　　　(3) County:

6. ☐ **I declare** under penalty of perjury under the laws of the State of California that the foregoing is true and correct.
7. ☐ **I am a California sheriff, marshal, or constable and** I certify that the foregoing is true and correct.

▶

Date:

_____
(SIGNATURE)

Form Adopted by Rule 982
Judicial Council of California
982(a)(23) [New July 1, 1987]

PROOF OF SERVICE
(Summons)

Code Civ. Proc., § 417.10(f)

NAME, ADDRESS, AND TELEPHONE NUMBER
OF ATTORNEY(S)

ATTORNEY(S)

SUPERIOR COURT OF CALIFORNIA, COUNTY OF

In the Matter of the Adoption Petition of	CASE NUMBER
_____ Adopting Parent(s)	**AFFIDAVIT/CERTIFICATE/DECLARATION RE MILITARY SERVICE** In adoption and related matters

STATE OF CALIFORNIA, COUNTY OF
I, ... say:
    (affiant's name)

I am (not)* a party to this proceeding
I reside at ....
My occupation is ....
I personally (know) (do not know)* the citee ....
              (name of citee - including aliases)

....
I have known said citee ....
          (approximate period of time)

The present known address of said citee is ....
....
The occupation of said citee is ....
The name of said citee's employer is ....
....
I last saw citee on .... day of .... , 19 ....
The approximate age of said citee is .... years.
The known physical incapacity of said citee is ....
....

*(Strike out inappropriate words.)

  Other known facts tending to show said citee is not in military service are:

(See Reverse Side)

AFFIDAVIT/CERTIFICATE/DECLARATION RE MILITARY SERVICE
In adoption and related matters

I (know) (have been unable to determine whether)* said citee (is) (is not)* in military service on active duty as a member of the Army of the United States, or of the United States Navy, or of the United States Marine Corps, or of the United States Coast Guard, or of any Department of the United States Air Force.

---

* *(Strike out inappropriate words.)*

AFFIDAVIT**

Dated: _____ , 19

Subscribed and sworn to before me

Dated: _____ , 19

_____
Notary Public in and for the County of
, State of California

DECLARATION**

I certify (or declare) under penalty of perjury that the foregoing is true and correct

Executed at _____ , California

Dated: _____ , 19

_____
Signature of Declarant

**This form is designed for use either as an affidavit or an unsworn statement made under penalty of perjury. If an affidavit, affiant should sign where indicated at the left. If an unsworn statement, he should sign where indicated at the right. DECLARATION TO BE SIGNED ONLY IF DECLARANT IS WITHIN THE STATE OF CALIFORNIA.*

NOTE 1: "Any person who shall make or use an affidavit (or declaration) required under this section knowing it to be false shall be guilty of a misdemeanor and shall be punishable by imprisonment not to exceed one year or by fine not to exceed $1,000 or both." Soldiers' and Sailors' Civil Relief Act of 1940, as amended.

NOTE 2: Certificates may be obtained from each of the Armed Services for a fee by writing the following branches; United States Air Force, Department of the Army, United States Marine Corps and United States Coast Guard. The correct addresses for inquiry may be obtained from the local offices of these branches.

If five (5) reports from the Military Service have been received, attach same to this affidavit/declaration.

ATTORNEY OR PARTY WITHOUT ATTORNEY *(Name and Address)*:

TELEPHONE NO.:

FOR COURT USE ONLY

C-116

ATTORNEY FOR *(Name)*:

NAME OF COURT:

STREET ADDRESS:

MAILING ADDRESS:

CITY AND ZIP CODE:

BRANCH NAME:

PLAINTIFF/PETITIONER:

DEFENDANT/RESPONDENT:

DECLARATION

CASE NUMBER:

I declare under penalty of perjury under the laws of the State of California that the foregoing is true and correct.

Date:

. . . .
(TYPE OR PRINT NAME)

▶ _____
(SIGNATURE OF DECLARANT)

☐ Petitioner/Plaintiff ☐ Respondent/Defendant ☐ Attorney

☐ Other *(specify)*:

(See reverse for a form to be used if this declaration will be attached to another court form before filing)

Form Approved by the
Judicial Council of California
MC-030 [New January 1, 1987]

DECLARATION

PLAINTIFF/PETITIONER:		CASE NUMBER:
DEFENDANT/RESPONDENT:		

This form must be attached to another form or court paper before it can be filed in court.

Form Approved by the
Judicial Council of California
MC-031 [New January 1, 1987]

ATTACHED DECLARATION

I declare under penalty of perjury under the laws of the State of California that the foregoing is true and correct.

Date:

. . . .

(TYPE OR PRINT NAME)   ▶   (SIGNATURE OF DECLARANT)

☐ Petitioner/Plaintiff ☐ Respondent/Defendant ☐ Attorney
☐ Other *(specify):*

(See reverse for a form to be used if this declaration is not to be attached to another court paper before filing)

INDEX

A

Abandonment hearing, 6/10, 6/25

Abandonment of child, by missing parent, 3/3-4, 6/1-36; definition, 3/3

Abandonment Order, 6/25, 6/26-27, 6/30; sample, 6/26-27

Abandonment Petition, 6/2, 6/7-9; sample, 6/7-8

Absent parent: consenting to adoption, 3/1, 4/1-25; contesting adoption, 3/7; definition, 2/6; locating, 3/2-7, 5/12-15; notifying of intended adoption, 5/5-10; refusal to consent to adoption, 3/7-8; rights lost with adoption, 2/2

Additional notice period, 5/23

Adoption: based on abandonment by absent parent, 3/3-4, 6/1-36; based on parent's willful failure to support child, 3/2-3, 3/4, 3/8, 5/1-40; based on termination of parental rights of absent father, 3/5-6, 7/1-29; consequences, 2/1-2; process, 2/6-15, 4/1-25; requirements, 2/3-5

Adoption agreement: consent adoption, 4/15, 4/16-17; samples, 4/16-17, 5/33-34, 7/24-25; termination of rights adoption, 7/24-25; willful failure adoption, 5/33-34

Adoption Certificate, 4/21

Adoption decree: abandonment adoption, 6/25, 6/28-30; consent adoption, 4/15, 4/18-19, 4/21; samples, 4/18-19, 5/31-32, 6/28-29, 7/22-23; setting aside, 2/2; termination of rights adoption, 7/22-23; willful failure adoption, 5/31-32

Adoption hearing: abandonment adoption, 6/10, 6/25; consent adoption, 4/14-15, 4/20-21; termination of rights adoption, 7/21; willful failure adoption, 5/23, 5/30-36

Adoption petition: abandonment adoption, 6/2, 6/3-5, 6/9; consent adoption, 4/4-6; samples, 2/12-13, 4/5-6, 5/2-3, 6/3-5, 7/3-4;

termination of rights adoption, 7/2-4; willful failure adoption, 5/1-4

Adult, adoption of, 1/2

Affidavit/Certificate/Declaration re Military Service. *See* Declaration re Military Service

Allegations, in adoption petition, 4/7-8

Alleged father, 3/5, 4/2. *See also* Out-of-wedlock births

Appeal, of Social Services Department assessment, 2/3n

Application and Declaration—Publication of Citation: abandonment adoption, 6/10, 6/14-15, 6/17; samples, 5/17-19, 6/14-15, 7/10-11; termination of rights adoption, 7/9, 7/10-11; willful failure adoption, 5/16-20

Assessment, by Social Service Department, 2/9, 3/8, 4/8-10, 5/4-5; appeal, 2/3n

Attorneys. *See* Lawyers

Aunt(s), notifying in abandonment adoption, 6/17-24

B

Birth certificate, amending, 2/15, 4/21, 4/23

Brother(s), notifying in abandonment adoption, 6/17-24

C

Case number, on adoption petition, 4/8

Certified copies, of personal documents, 2/7-8

Checklists: abandonment adoption, 6/30-36; consent adoption, 4/23-25; Los Angeles County, 4/25, 5/39-40, 6/34-36, 7/28-29; termination of rights adoption, 7/26-29; willful failure adoption, 5/36-40

Citation to Appear: abandonment adoption, 6/10, 6/11-13, 6/17; samples, 5/22, 6/11-13, 7/14-15; termination of rights adoption, 7/9, 7/14-15; willful failure adoption, 5/16, 5/20, 5/22

CATALOG
...more books from Nolo Press

Estate Planning & Probate

Plan Your Estate
Attorney Denis Clifford. National 2nd ed.
Covers every significant aspect of estate planning and gives detailed, specific instructions for preparing a living trust. Includes all the tear-out forms and step-by-step instructions to let you prepare an estate plan designed for your special needs. Good in all states except Louisiana.
$19.95/NEST

Make Your Own Living Trust
Attorney Denis Clifford. National 1st ed.
Find out how a living trust works, how to create one, and how to determine what kind of trust is right for you. Contains all the forms and instructions you need to prepare a basic living trust to avoid probate, a marital life estate trust (A-B trust) to avoid probate and estate taxes, and a back-up will. Good in all states except Louisiana.
$19.95/LITR

Nolo's Simple Will Book
Attorney Denis Clifford. National 2nd ed.
It's easy to write a legally valid will using this book. Includes all the instructions and sample forms you need to name a personal guardian for minor children, leave property to minor children or young adults and update a will when necessary. Good in all states except Louisiana.
$17.95/SWIL

Who Will Handle Your Finances if You Can't?
Attorneys Denis Clifford & Mary Randolph. National 1st ed.
Give a trusted person legal authority to handle your financial matters if illness or old age makes it impossible for you to handle them yourself. Create a durable power of attorney for finances with the step-by-step instructions and fill-in-the-blank forms included in this book.
$19.95/FINA

The Conservatorship Book
Lisa Goldoftas & Attorney Carolyn Farren. California 1st ed.
Provides forms and all instructions necessary to file conservatorship documents, appear in court, be appointed conservator and end a conservatorship.
$24.95/CNSV

How to Probate an Estate
Julia Nissley. California 7th ed.
Save costly attorneys' fees by handling the probate process yourself. This book shows you step-by-step how to settle an estate. It also explains the simple procedures you can use to transfer assets that don't require probate. Forms included.
$34.95/PAE

LAW FORM KITS

Nolo's Law Form Kit: Wills
Attorney Denis Clifford & Lisa Goldoftas. National 1st ed.
All the forms and instructions you need to create a legally valid will, quickly and easily.
$14.95/KWL

AUDIO CASSETTE TAPES

Write Your Will
Attorney Ralph Warner with Joanne Greene. National 1st ed. 60 minutes
This tape answers the most frequently asked questions about writing a will and covers all key issues.
$14.95/TWYW

5 Ways to Avoid Probate
Attorney Ralph Warner with Joanne Greene National 1st ed. 60 minutes
Provides clear, in-depth explanations of the principal probate avoidance techniques.
$14.95/TPRO

SOFTWARE

WillMaker®
Version 5.0

Make your own legal will and living will (healthcare directive)—and thoroughly document your final arrangements—with WillMaker 5. WillMaker's easy-to-use in-terview format takes you through each document step-by-step. On-line legal help is available throughout the program. Name a guardian for your children, make up to 100 property bequests, direct your healthcare in the event of coma or terminal ill ness, and let your loved ones know your wishes around your own final arrangements. Good in all states except Louisiana
WINDOWS $69.95/WIW5
DOS $69.95/WI5
MACINTOSH $69.95/WM5

Nolo's Personal RecordKeeper
Version 3.0

Finally, a safe, accessible place for your important records. Over 200 categories and subcategories to organize and store your important financial, legal and personal information, compute your net worth and create inventories for insurance records. Export your net worth and home inventory data to Quicken®.
DOS $49.95/FRI3
MACINTOSH $49.95/FRM3

Nolo's Living Trust
Version 1.0

Put your assets into a trust and save your heirs the headache, time and expense of probate with this easy-to-use software. Use it to set up an individual or shared marital trust, transfer property to the trust, and change or revoke the trust at any time. Its manual guides you through the process, and legal help screens and an on-line glossary explain key legal terms and concepts. Good in all states except Louisiana.
MACINTOSH $79.95/LTM1

Represent Yourself in Court: How to Prepare & Try a Winning Case
Attorneys Paul Bergman & Sara Berman-Barrett
National 1st ed.
Handle your own civil court case from start to finish without a lawyer with the most thorough guide to contested court cases ever published for the non-lawyer. Covers all aspects of civil trials including lining up persuasive witnesses, presenting testimony, cross-examining witnesses and even picking a jury.
$29.95/RYC

Fight Your Ticket
Attorney David Brown. California 5th ed.
Shows you how to fight an unfair traffic ticket—when you're stopped, at arraignment, at trial and on appeal.
$18.95/FYT

Everybody's Guide to Small Claims Court
Attorney Ralph Warner.
National 5th ed.. California 11th ed.
These books will help you decide if you should sue in Small Claims Court, show you how to file and serve papers, tell you what to bring to court and how to collect a judgment.
National $16.95/NSCC
California $16.95/CSCC

Everybody's Guide to Municipal Court
Judge Roderic Duncan. California 1st ed.
Sue and defend cases for up to $25,000 in California Municipal Court. Step-by-step instructions for preparing and filing forms, gathering evidence and appearing in court.
$29.95/MUNI

Collect Your Court Judgment
Gini Graham Scott, Attorney Stephen Elias & Lisa Goldoftas. California 2nd ed.
Contains step-by-step instructions and all the forms you need to collect a court judgment from the debtor's bank accounts, wages, business receipts, real estate or other assets.
$19.95/JUDG

How to Change Your Name
Attorneys David Loeb & David Brown. California 5th ed.
All the forms and instructions you need to change your name in California.
$19.95/NAME

The Criminal Records Book
Attorney Warren Siegel. California 3rd ed.
Shows you step-by-step how to seal criminal records, dismiss convictions, destroy marijuana records and reduce felony convictions.
$19.95/CRIM

Winning in Small Claims Court
Attorney Ralph Warner with Joanne Greene.
National 1st ed. 60 minutes
Strategies for preparing and presenting a winning small claims court case.
$14.95/TWIN

The Legal Guide for Starting & Running a Small Business
Attorney Fred S. Steingold. National 1st ed.
An essential resource for every small business owner. Find out how to form a sole proprietorship, partnership or corporation, negotiate a favorable lease, hire and fire employees, write contracts and resolve disputes.
$22.95/RUNS

Sexual Harassment on the Job: What it is and How To Stop it.
Attorneys William Petrocelli & Barbara Kate Repa.
National 1st ed.
An invaluable resource for both employees experiencing harassment and employers interested in creating a policy against sexual harassment and a procedure for handling complaints.
$14.95/HARS

Marketing Without Advertising
Michael Phillips & Salli Rasberry. National 1st ed.
Outlines practical steps for building and expanding a small business without spending a lot of money on advertising.
$14.00/MWAD

Your Rights in the Workplace
Barbara Kate Repa. National 2nd ed.
The first comprehensive guide to workplace rights —from hiring to firing. Covers wages and overtime, parental leave, unemployment and disability insurance, worker's compensation, job safety, discrimination and illegal firings and layoffs.
$15.95/YRW

How to Write a Business Plan
Mike McKeever. National 4th ed.
This book will show you how to write the business plan and loan package necessary to finance your business and make it work.
$19.95/SBS

The Partnership Book
Attorneys Denis Clifford & Ralph Warner.
National 4th ed.
Shows you step-by-step how to write a solid partnership agreement that meets your needs. It covers initial contributions to the business, wages, profit-sharing, buy-outs, death or retirement of a partner and disputes.
$24.95/PART

Software Development: A Legal Guide
Book with Disk-DOS
Attorney Stephen Fishman
National 1st ed.
A reference bible for people in the software industry. This book explores the legal ins and outs of copyright, trade secret and patent protection, employment agreement, working with independent contractors and employees, development and publishing agreement and multi-media development. All contracts and agreements included on disk.
$44.95/SFT

How to Form a Nonprofit Corporation
Attorney Anthony Mancuso.
National 1st ed.
Explains the legal formalities involved and provides detailed information on the differences in the law among all 50 states. It also contains forms for the Articles, Bylaws and Minutes you need, along with complete instructions for obtaining federal 501(c)(3) tax exemptions and qualifying for public charity status.
$24.95/NNP

The California Nonprofit Corporation Handbook
Attorney Anthony Mancuso.
California 6th ed.
Shows you step-by-step how to form and operate a nonprofit corporation in California. It includes the latest corporate and tax law changes, and the forms for the Articles, Bylaws and Minutes.
$29.95/NON

How to Form Your Own Corporation
Attorney Anthony Mancuso
California 7th ed.. New York 2nd ed..
Texas 4th ed.. Florida 3rd ed.
These books contain the forms, instructions and tax information you need to incorporate a small business yourself and save hundreds of dollars in lawyers' fees.
California $29.95/CCOR
New York $24.95/NYCO
Texas $29.95/TCOR
How to Form Your Own Corporation is also available with incorporation forms on disk for these states:
New York 1st ed. DOS $39.95/NYCI, Mac. $39.95/NYCM
Texas 4th ed. DOS $39.95/TCI
Florida 3rd ed. DOS $39.95/FCCO

The California Professional Corporation Handbook
Attorney Anthony Mancuso.
California 5th ed.
Health care professionals, lawyers, accountants and members of certain other professions must fulfill special requirements when forming a corporation in California. Contains up-to-date tax information plus all the forms and instructions necessary.
$34.95/PROF

The Independent Paralegal's Handbook

Attorney Ralph Warner.
National 2nd ed.
Provides legal and business guidelines for anyone who wants to go into business as an independent paralegal helping consumers with routine legal tasks.
$24.95 PARA

AUDIO CASSETTE TAPES

Getting Started as an Independent Paralegal

Attorney Ralph Warner. National 2nd ed.
Two tapes, approximately 2 hours
Practical and legal advice on going into business as an independent paralegal from the author of *The Independent Paralegal's Handbook.*
$44.95/GSIP

How to Start Your Own Business: Small Business Law

Attorney Ralph Warner with Joanne Greene. National 1st ed. 60 minutes
What every small business owner needs to know about organizing as a sole proprietorship, partnership or corporation, protecting the business name, renting space, hiring employees and paying taxes.
$14.95/TBUS

SOFTWARE

Nolo's Partnership Maker

Version 1.0
Attorney Tony Mancuso & Michael Radtke
Prepare a legal partnership agreement for doing business in any state. Select and assemble the standard partnership clauses provided or create your own customized agreement. Includes on-line legal help screens, glossary and tutorial, and a manual that takes you through the process step-by-step.
DOS $129.95/PAGI1

California Incorporator

Version 1.0 (good only in CA)
Attorney Tony Mancuso
Answer the questions on the screen and this software program will print out the 35-40 pages of documents you need to make your California corporation legal. A 200-page manual explains the incorporation process.
DOS $129.00/INCI
DOS $39.95 TCI
MACINTOSH $39.95 TCM

Florida 3rd Ed.
DOS 3-1/2 $39.95/FLCO

The Neighborhood

Neighbor Law: Fences, Trees, Boundaries & Noise

Attorney Cora Jordan. National 1st ed.
Answers common questions about the subjects that most often trigger disputes between neighbors: fences, trees, boundaries and noise. It explains how to find the law and resolve disputes without a nasty lawsuit.
$14.95/NEI

Safe Homes, Safe Neighborhoods: Stopping Crime Where You Live

Stephanie Mann with M.C. Blakeman. National 1st ed.
Learn how you and your neighbors can work together to protect yourselves, your families and property from crime. Explains how to form a neighborhood crime prevention group; avoid burglaries, muggings and rapes; combat gangs and drug dealing; improve home security and make the neighborhood safer for children.
$14.95/SAFE

Dog Law

Attorney Mary Randolph. National 1st ed.
A practical guide to the laws that affect dog owners and their neighbors. Answers common questions about biting, barking, veterinarians and more.
$12.95/DOG

Money Matters

Stand Up to the IRS

Attorney Fred Daily. National 2nd ed.
Gives detailed strategies on surviving an audit, appealing an audit decision, going to Tax Court and dealing with IRS collectors. It also discusses filing delinquent tax returns, tax crimes, concerns of small business people and getting help from the IRS ombudsman.
$21.95/SIRS

How to File for Bankruptcy

Attorneys Stephen Elias,
Albin Renauer & Robin Leonard. National 4th ed.
Trying to decide whether or not filing for bankruptcy makes sense? This book contains an overview of the process and all the forms plus step-by-step instructions you need to file for Chapter 7 Bankruptcy.
$25.95/HFB

Money Troubles: Legal Strategies to Cope with Your Debts

Attorney Robin Leonard. National 2nd ed.
Essential for anyone who has gotten behind on bills. It shows how to obtain a credit file, negotiate with persistent creditors, challenge wage attachments, contend with repossessions and more.
$16.95/MT

Simple Contracts for Personal Use

Attorney Stephen Elias & Marcia Stewart.
National 2nd ed.
Contains clearly written legal form contracts to buy and sell property, borrow and lend money, store and lend personal property, release others from personal liability, or pay a contractor to do home repairs. Includes agreements to arrange child care and other household help.
$16.95/CONT

LAW FORM KITS

Nolo's Law Form Kit: Personal Bankruptcy

Attorneys Steve Elias, Albin Renauer & Robin Leonard and Lisa Goldoftas. National 1st ed.
All the forms and instructions you need to file for Chapter 7 bankruptcy.
$14.95/KBNK

Nolo's Law Forms Kit: Rebuild Your Credit

Attorney Robin Leonard. National 1st ed.
Provides strategies for dealing with debts and rebuilding your credit. Shows you how to negotiate with creditors and collection agencies, clean up your credit file, devise a spending plan and get credit in your name.
$14.95/KCRD

Nolo's Law Form Kit: Power of Attorney

Attorneys Denis Clifford & Mary Randolph and Lisa Goldoftas.
National 1st ed.
Create a conventional power of attorney to assign someone you trust to take of your finances, business, real estate or children when you are away or unavailable. Provides all the forms with step-by-step instructions.
$14.95/KPA

Nolo's Law Form Kit: Loan Agreements

Attorney Stephen Elias, Marcia Stewart & Lisa Goldoftas.
National 1st ed.
Provides all the forms and instructions necessary to create a legal and effective promissory note. Shows how to decide on an interest rate, set a payment schedule and keep track of payments.
$14.95/KLOAN

Nolo's Law Form Kit: Buy and Sell Contracts

Attorney Stephen Elias, Marcia Stewart & Lisa Goldoftas.
National 1st ed.
Step-by-step instructions and all the forms necessary for creating bills of sale for cars, boats, computers, electronic equipment, and other personal property.
$9.95/K CONT

Family Matters

Nolo's Pocket Guide to Family Law

Attorneys Robin Leonard & Stephen Elias. Nat, 3rd ed.
Here's help for anyone who has a question or problem involving family law—marriage, divorce, adoption or living together.
$14.95/FLD

Divorce & Money

Violet Woodhouse & Victoria Felton-Collins with M.C. Blakeman.
National 2nd ed.
Explains how to evaluate such major assets as family homes and businesses, investments, pensions, and how to arrive at a division of property that is fair to both sides.
$21.95/DIMO

The Living Together Kit

Attorneys Toni Ihara & Ralph Warner. National 6th ed.
A detailed guide designed to help the increasing number of unmarried couples living together understand the laws that affect them. Sample agreements and instructions are included.
$17.95/LTK

A Legal Guide for Lesbian and Gay Couples

Attorneys Hayden Curry, Denis Clifford & Robin Leonard. National 7th ed.
This book shows lesbian and gay couples how to write a living-together contract, plan for medical emergencies, understand the practical and legal aspects of having and raising children and plan their estates. Includes forms and sample agreements.
$21.95/LG

California Marriage & Divorce Law

Attorneys Ralph Warner, Toni Ihara & Stephen Elias. California 11th ed.
Explains community property, pre-nuptial contracts, foreign marriages, buying a house, getting a divorce, dividing property, and more. Pre-nuptial contracts included.
$19.95/MARR

Divorce: A New Yorker's Guide to Doing it Yourself

Bliss Alexandra. New York 1st ed.
Step-by-step instructions and all the forms you need to do your own divorce and save thousands of dollars in legal fees. Shows you how to divide property, arrange custody of the children, set child support and maintenance (alimony), draft a divorce agreement and fill out and file all forms.
$24.95/NYDIV

How to Raise or Lower Child Support in California

Judge Roderic Duncan & Attorney Warren Siegal. California 1st ed.
Appropriate for parents on either side of the support issue. All the forms and instructions necessary to raise or lower an existing child support order.
$16.95/CHLD

The Guardianship Book

Lisa Goldoftas & Attorney David Brown. California 1st ed.
Provides step-by-step instructions and the forms needed to obtain a legal guardianship of a minor without a lawyer.
$19.95/GB

How to Do Your Own Divorce

Attorney Charles Sherman
(Texas ed. by Sherman & Simons)
California 19th ed. & Texas 5th ed.
These books contain all the forms and instructions you need to do your own uncontested divorce without a lawyer.
California $21,95/CDIV
Texas $17.95/TDIV

Practical Divorce Solutions

Attorney Charles Sherman.
California 2nd ed.
Covers the emotional aspects of divorce and provides an overview of the legal and financial considerations.
$12.95/PDS

How to Adopt Your Stepchild in California

Frank Zagone & Attorney Mary Randolph.
California 4th ed.
Provides sample forms and step-by-step instructions for completing a simple uncontested stepparent adoption in California.
$22.95/ADOP

Patent, Copyright & Trademark

Trademark: How to Name Your Business & Product

Attorneys Kate McGrath & Stephen Elias, With Trademark Attorney Sarah Shena. National 1st ed.
Learn how to choose a name or logo that others can't copy, conduct a trademark search, register a trademark with the U.S. Patent and Trademark Office and protect and maintain the trademark.
$29.95/TRD

Patent It Yourself

Attorney David Pressman.
National 3rd ed.
From the patent search to the actual application, this book covers everything including the use and licensing of patents, successful marketing and how to deal with infringement.
$36.95/PAT

The Inventor's Notebook

Fred Grissom & Attorney David Pressman.
National 1st ed.
Helps you document the process of successful independent inventing by providing forms, instructions, references to relevant areas of patent law, a bibliography of legal and non-legal aids and more.
$19.95/INOT

The Copyright Handbook

Attorney Stephen Fishman.
National 1st ed.
Provides forms and step-by-step instructions for protecting all types of written expression under U.S. and international copyright law. Covers copyright infringement, fair use, works for hire and transfers of copyright ownership.
$24.95/COHA

Landlords & Tenants

The Landlord's Law Book, Vol. 1: Rights & Responsibilities

Attorneys David Brown & Ralph Warner.
California 4th ed.
Essential for every California landlord. Covers deposits, leases and rental agreements, inspections (tenants' privacy rights), habitability (rent withholding), ending a tenancy, liability and rent control. Forms included.
$32.95/LBRT

The Landlord's Law Book, Vol. 2: Evictions

Attorney David Brown. California 4th ed.
Show step-by-step how to go to court and evict a tenant. Contains all the tear-out forms and necessary instructions.
$32.95/LBEV

Tenants' Rights

Attorneys Myron Moskovitz & Ralph Warner.
California 11th ed.
This practical guide to dealing with your landlord explains your rights under federal law, California law and rent control ordinances. Forms included.
$15.95/CTEN

Homeowners

How to Buy a House in California

Attorney Ralph Warner, Ira Serkes & George Devine.
California 2nd ed.
Effective strategies for finding a house, working with a real estate agent, making an offer and negotiating intelligently. Includes information on all types of mortgages as well as private financing options.
$19.95/BHCA

For Sale By Owner

George Devine. California 2nd ed.
Everything you need to know to sell your own house, from pricing and marketing, to writing a contract and going through escrow. Disclosure and contract forms included.
$24.95/FSBO

Homestead Your House

Attorneys Ralph Warner, Charles Sherman & Toni Ihara. California 8th ed.
Shows you how to file a Declaration of Homestead and includes complete instructions and tear-out forms.
$9.95/HOME

The Deeds Book

Attorney Mary Randolph.
California 2nd ed.
Shows you how to fill out and file the right kind of deed when transferring property. Outlines the legal requirements of real property transfer.
$15.95/DEED

LAW FORM KITS

Nolo's Law form Kit: Leases & Rental Agreements

Attorney Ralph Warner & Marcia Stewart
California 1st ed.
With these easy-to-use forms and instructions, California landlords can prepare their own rental application, fixed term lease and month -to-month rental agreement.
$14.95/KLEAS

Just For Fun

Devil's Advocates:
The Unnatural History of Lawyers

by Andrew & Jonathan Roth. National 1st ed.
A hilarious look at the history of the legal profession.
$12.95/DA

29 Reasons Not to Go to Law School

Attorneys Ralph Warner & Toni Ihara. National 3rd ed.
Filled with humor, this book can save you three years, $70,000 and your sanity.
$9.95/29R

Poetic Justice: The Funniest, Meanest Things Ever Said About Lawyers

Edited by Jonathan & Andrew Roth. National 1st ed.
A great gift for anyone in the legal profession who has managed to maintain a sense of humor.
$8.95/PJ

Nolo's Favorite Lawyer Jokes on Disk

Over 200 jokes and hilariously nasty remarks about lawyers. 100% guaranteed to produce an evening of chuckles and drive every lawyer you know nuts.
DOS 3-1/2 $9.95/JODI
MACINTOSH $9.95/JODM

Older Americans

Beat the Nursing Home Trap:
A Consumer's Guide to Choosing and Financing Long-Term Care
(formerly Elder Care)

Joseph Matthews. National 2nd ed.
This practical guide shows how to protect assets, arrange home health care, find nursing and non-nursing home residences, evaluate nursing home insurance and understand Medicare, Medicaid and other benefit programs.
$18.95/ELD

Social Security, Medicare & Pensions

Attorney Joseph Matthews with Dorothy Matthews Berman. National 5th ed.
Offers invaluable guidance through the current maze of rights and benefits for those 55 and over, including Medicare, Medicaid and Social Security retirement and disability benefits, and age discrimination protections.
$15.95/SOA

Research & Reference

Legal Research: How to Find and Understand the Law

Attorneys Stephen Elias & Susan Levinkind. National 3rd ed.
A valuable tool on its own or as a companion to just about every other Nolo book. Gives easy-to-use, step-by-step instructions on how to find legal information.
$19.95/LRES

Legal Research Made Easy: A Roadmap Through the Law Library Maze

2-1/2 hr. videotape and 40-page manual
Nolo Press/Legal Star Communications. National 1st ed.
Professor Bob Berring explains how to use all the basic legal research tools in your local law library with an easy-to-follow six-step research plan and a sense of humor.
$89.95/LRME

Consumer

Nolo's Pocket Guide to California Law

Attorney Lisa Guerin & Nolo Press Editors.
California 2nd ed.
Get quick clear answers to questions about child support, custody, consumer rights, employee rights, government benefits, divorce, bankruptcy, adoption, wills and much more.
$10.95/CLAW

Nolo's Pocket Guide to Consumer Rights

Barbara Kaufman.
California 2nd ed.
Practical advice on hundreds of consumer topics. Shows Californians how and where to complain about everything from accountants, misleading advertisements and lost baggage to vacation scams and dishonored warranties.
$14.95/CAG

Legal Breakdown:
40 Ways to Fix Our Legal System

Nolo Press Editors & Staff.
National 1st ed.
Forty common-sense proposals to make our legal system fairer, faster, cheaper and more accessible.
$8.95/LEG

How to Win Your Personal Injury Claim

Attorney Joseph Matthews. National 1st ed.
Armed with the right information anyone can handle a personal injury claim. This step-by-step guide shows you how to avoid insurance company run-arounds, evaluate what your claim is worth, obtain a full and fair settlement and save for yourself what you would pay a lawyer.
$24.95/PICL

LAW FORM KITS

Nolo's Law Form Kit:
Hiring Child Care & Household Help

Attorney Barbara Kate Repa & Lisa Goldoftas
National 1st ed.
All the necessary forms and instructions for fulfilling your legal and tax responsibilities. Includes employment contracts, applications forms and required IRS forms.
$14.95/KCHLD

Immigration

How to Get a Green Card:
Legal Ways to Stay in the U.S.A.

Attorney Loida Nicolas Lewis with Len T. Madlanscay.
National 1st ed.
Written by a former INS attorney, this book clearly explains the steps involved in getting a green card. It covers who can qualify, what documents to present, and how to fill out all the forms and have them processed. Tear-out forms included.
$19.95/GRN

order form

CODE	QUANTITY	ITEM	UNIT PRICE	TOTAL
			Subtotal	
			California residents add Sales Tax	
		Shipping & Handling ($4 for 1 item; $5 for 2-3 items; +$.50 each additional item	
		2nd day UPS (additional $5; $8 in Alaska & Hawaii)	
			TOTAL	

Name

Address (UPS to street address; Priority Mail to P.O. boxes)

FOR FASTER SERVICE, USE YOUR CREDIT CARD AND OUR TOLL-FREE NUMBERS

Monday-Friday, 8am to 5pm Pacific Time
ORDER LINE   1-800-992-6656   in 510 area, call 549-1976
CUSTOMER SERVICE   1-510-549-1976
FAX YOUR ORDER   1-800-645-0895   in 510 area, call 548-5902

METHOD OF PAYMENT

☐ Check enclosed   ☐ VISA   ☐ Mastercard   ☐ Discover Card   ☐ American Express

Account #   Expiration Date

Authorizing Signature   Daytime Phone

SEND TO

Nolo Press, 950 Parker Street, Berkeley, CA 94710
Allow 2-3 weeks for delivery. PRICES SUBJECT TO CHANGE.

visit our store in Berkeley

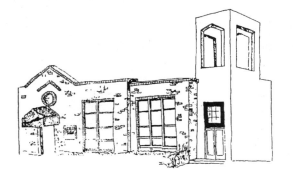

If you live in the Bay Area, be sure to visit the Nolo Press Bookstore
on the corner of 9th & Parker Streets in west Berkeley. You'll find
our complete line of books and software—all at a discount.

Call 1-510-704-2248 for hours.   ADOP 4